The Spam Letters

THE SPAM LETTERS

Jonathan Land

**NO STARCH
PRESS**

Printed on recycled paper in the United States of America
1 2 3 4 5 6 7 8 9 10—07 06 05 04

No Starch Press and the No Starch Press logo are registered trademarks of No Starch Press, Inc. Other product and company names mentioned herein may be the trademarks of their respective owners. Rather than use a trademark symbol with every occurrence of a trademarked name, we are using the names only in an editorial fashion and to the benefit of the trademark owner, with no intention of infringement of the trademark.

Publisher: William Pollock
Managing Editor: Karol Jurado
Cover and Interior Design: Octopod Studios
Copyeditor: Andy Carroll
Composition: Wedobooks
Proofreader: Stephanie Provines

For information on translations or book distributors, please contact No Starch Press, Inc. directly:

No Starch Press, Inc.
555 De Haro Street, Suite 250, San Francisco, CA 94107
phone: 415-863-9900; fax: 415-863-9950; info@nostarch.com; http://www.nostarch.com

Library of Congress Cataloging-in-Publication Data

Land, Jonathan.
   The spam letters / Jonathan Land.
        p. cm.
  1. Internet--Humor. 2. Unsolicited electronic mail messages--Humor.
I. Title.
   PN6231.I62 L36 2004
   816'.6--dc22

                                                    2003024731

Contents

Acknowledgments   **ix**

Foreword   **xi**

Preface: About the Letters   **xiii**

CHAPTER 1: Introduction   1

Subject: Re: process printed labels, printed bags and packaging   1

CHAPTER 2: Products for Prey: Part 1   5

Subject: Re: Hottest Gadget - Rc mini cars limited time   6

Subject: Re: Don't lose your remote cotrol again!   10

Subject: Re: At Last, Herbal V, the All Natural Alternative is Available!   12

Subject: Re: Open Any Lock with Kwick Pick - On Sale Today!   14

Subject: Re: Take Pringles' Spicy Quiz!   16

Subject: Re: Cheap Cigarettes Online   17

Subject: Re: Save on Shipping Tape...Stretch Film...Bubble   18

Subject: Re: Natural Viagra 12154   20

Subject: Re: Sexual Enhancement & FREE Herbs!   23

Subject: Re: BURN-OFF BODY FAT QUICK AND EASY!   24

CHAPTER 3: Foreign Affairs: Part 1   27

My Buddy Kutty   **28**

Subject: Re: trade enquiry   28

Subject: Re: SAMPLES ATTACHMENTS; i   29

Subject: Re: re-enquiry- ii   32

Subject: Re: SAMPLES ATTACHMENTS; i   33

Subject: s.kutty sent you a Greeting   35
Subject: Copy of your Greeting   36
Help Unwanted   **37**
Subject: Re: job application   37
Subject: Re: Re: job application   38
Subject: Re: Re: Re: job application   39
Penitentiary Pants   **41**
Subject: RE: THE MANAGING DIRECTOR   41
Subject: Re: textil   43
Subject: Re: THE MANAGING DIRECTOR   46
Subject: Re: THE MANAGING DIRECTOR   47
Subject: Re: Your mail Dated Dec 04, 2001   49
Subject: Re: Re: Re: Re: job application   50
Subject: Re: Re: perumal-jordan   51
Subject: Re: Re: Re: perumal-jordan   52
Subject: Re: Re: Re: Re: perumal-jordan   55
Subject: Re: Re: Re: Re: Re: perumal-jordan   56
Subject: Re: Re: Re: Re: Re: Re: perumal-jordan   58

CHAPTER 4: Spam Potpourri: Part 1   **59**
Subject: Re: Dear JONATHAN, Pizza Hut asks you   60
Subject: Re: Special Character Costume Source;
     discount Magic Supply source   61
Subject: Re: Business Development for ehandjob.org   62
Subject: Re: Snowhite and the Seven Dwarfs - The REAL story!   65
Subject: Re: U.S. Immigration Online   67
Subject: Re: Info For You   71

CHAPTER 5: A Quick Buck   **73**
Subject: Re: Complimentary Disney Area Vacation   74
Subject: Re: The big ONE!   76
Subject: Re: Casting Call for Reality TV's Fastest New Show!   78
Subject: RE: Immediate Foreclosure Notice   80
Subject: Re: New Business Proposal   82
Subject: Re: Have you planned for your family's future? HRQ   84
Subject: Re: GUARANTEED ways to have more
     MONEY FOR THE HOLIDAYS!   86
Subject: Re: Swim with the dolphins 3693   87
Subject: Re: FUNDING   88
Subject: Re: Horse Running this Wednesday 03/04/02 at Ludlow   90

CHAPTER 6: Interlude: Bad Impressions   **93**
Subject: Re:Is Snoring Affecting Your Life?   94
Subject: Re: Software Development Solutions   95
Subject: Re: Looking for Actors, Models, Singers and Dancers!!   98

CHAPTER 7: Products for Prey: Part 2   **101**

Subject: Re: FEED THE BIRDS NOT THE SQUIRRELS!!   102

Subject: Re: I have found a weight loss product that really works.   104

Subject: Re: AFRAID OF CANCER   105

Subject: Re: Perfect Gift For Your Pastor or Church Secretary   107

Subject: Re: Christmas Gift   110

Subject: Re: Christmas Gift   111

Subject: Re: Hydrogen Peroxide from producer   112

Subject: Re: Are You a BOWLER? Check Out
    the HOTTEST NEW BOWLING BALL!   114

Subject: Re: New Pill makes your semen taste sweet
    -she'll swallow and love it   116

Subject: RE: The Stainless Steel Network   118

Subject: RE: The Stainless Steel Network   119

Subject: RE: The Stainless Steel Network   120

CHAPTER 8: Foreign Affairs: Part 2: Nigerian Scam Artists   **123**

Subject: Re: ASSISTANCE   124

Subject: Re: URGENT RESPONSE   130

Subject: Re: URGENT ASSISTANCE   132

Subject: Re: REQUEST FOR ASSISTANCE   134

Subject: Re: THINKING ABOUT IT   135

Subject: Re: CALL ME   136

Subject: Re: CALL ME   137

Subject: Re: act fast.   138

Subject: Re: CALL ME   139

Subject: Re: REALISE THE REALITY   140

Subject: Re: REALISE THE REALITY   141

Subject: Re: send info   142

Subject: Re: not complete   143

Subject: Re: Act fast.   144

Subject: Re: Act fast.   145

Subject: Re: joint partnership venture   145

Subject: Re: REALISE THE REALITY   147

Subject: Re: confidentaility   148

Subject: Re: confidentaility   149

Subject: Re: confidentaility   150

Subject: Re: URGENT ASSISTANCE   151

Subject: Re: URGENT   154

Subject: Re: URGENT   155

Subject: A Fantastic Proposal   157

Subject: Re: A Fantastic Proposal Reply   159

Subject: Re: RESPOND   160

CHAPTER 9: Sex Sells?   165

Subject: Re: Young College Chicks!   166

Subject: Re: VIDEOS OF BRITNEY SPEERS THAT YOU MUST SEE !'   166

Subject: Re: SCARE PEOPLE WITH YOUR HUGE COCK!   169

Subject: Re: DO YOU LIKE HARDCORE PORN?   170

Subject: Re: startfreesex open !   171

Subject: Re: Re: startfreesex open !   172

Subject: Re: Someone is interested in you   174

Subject: Re: meet me in the same place LKCKBU   176

Subject: Re: Incest Porn! 28043   178

Subject: Re: Watch Teen Farm Girls Have Sex
    with their animals Free! ltilwvaw   179

CHAPTER 10: Spam Potpourri: Part 2   183

Subject: Re: Upgrade to first class   184

Subject: Re: Interested In Listing Jonathan Land In Our New Directory   188

Subject: Subject: Re: Your Military Benefits are Waiting!   190

Subject: Re: yourish.com   192

Subject: Re: Aliens or Time Travelers PLEASE HELP!   193

Subject: Re: Own your own shopping mall!   196

Subject: Re: Your Child Can Read with Ease!   202

**Warning/Disclaimer: Do Not Try This at Home
(Or Anywhere Else You Have an Internet Connection)**   209

Acknowledgments

I'd like to thank the following people for the following things:

Spammers, for being a constant source of inspiration with their bounty of material. Now stop it. I have enough.

Paul and Irene Land, for being my parents.

Dick Stockton and Lesley Visser, for their support.

Jill Shuler, for first imagining the site as a book and wanting to come home to someone capable of writing the questionable material contained herein.

Everyone at No Starch Press, for publishing and working so hard on this book.

Joshua Freeman, for getting me together with No Starch.

Stephanie Cole, for advising me on how to avoid others' litigious nature (I hope).

l-dopa (particularly Jeff Hobbs and Joshua Newman), Kate Guttman, and mbv-1 (particularly Hélène de Grosbois), for ideas and feedback.

Iain Aitch, Kirsten Hamilton, and Ellis Hennican, for helping spread the good word and several bad ones.

Amber Brown, Kevin Dorn, Emilie Smith, Lauren Ryder, Aaron Mulvany, Danielle Friedland, Jennifer "Rivka" Magee, and the folks in Negativland for listening to my incessant whining about all of the humorless things involving a humor book.

and

All the people who forwarded me the juiciest spam from their inboxes.

Jonathan Land

Caldwell, NJ

Foreword

When I was first approached by Jonathan Land to write a foreword for his book, I thought to myself, "I'd like to meet this guy." Me and my Honey got in the car and started off on a little road trip. (Honey is the name of my shotgun.)

As I sat in a hotel bar thinking about things and hoping it wasn't karaoke night, I realized that by the time I tracked down Mr. Land, made him plead for his life, and drove back home, I could have sent out millions of e-mail solicitations and brought in some fast cash. That's right . . . I spam people.

After all, I'm just trying to make a buck, and so is this guy. Who am I to judge his annoying (if not quixotic) efforts? He's certainly not hurting my business any, and since I use fake e-mail addresses, it's not like he's bombarding me with mail. Some of his letters even made me laugh a little.

I'd like to point out that "spammers" are no different than anyone else. We put our pants on one leg at a time, the days we put on pants. It's a jungle out there, and we need to earn a living. Sure, some people might think that we prey on the elderly, and the stupid, but is it our fault that so many fools and their money are so easily parted? If people really think they can make their lives better through the products I'm pushing, then their problems have a much deeper root than I could possibly cause.

Sure it's not a noble business, but it exists because there's a demand for people like me to supply, and I'm doing very well, thank you.

I'd actually like to take this opportunity to thank Jonathan Land for finding me, and giving me this opportunity to try to make the voice of my people heard. After all, if you've bought this book, I know that you're too smart for me to hear from, and you won't be purchasing the wonderful combination pasta pots with a built-in colanders, Canadian pharmaceuticals, or free money I

claim to have to offer. I just want you to know I have a wife and kids to provide for. I'm unskilled, and this is the only way I can do it, and believe me,
you don't want these hands serving you fast food.

So I hope you enjoy *The Spam Letters*. I don't think I have a quarter as much
fun sending out the e-mails as Mr. Land does replying to them. I wish him
well. Really. As a matter of fact, if the book seems profitable enough, maybe
I'll start selling it for him with my particular methods. I'm sure the irony
will embarrass him greatly.

Name Withheld

Multi-Level Marketer

Preface:
About the Letters

I can't remember why I started writing back. . . .

Was I mad as hell and not taking it anymore?

Did my insatiable mean streak miss a feeding?

Did I see an opportunity to generate a few cheap laughs?

These all seem like viable reasons . . . but is writing ridiculous letters to mostly dead addresses and trying to lure the authors behind the functional ones into an increasingly absurd dialog justifiable?

I don't know. While I'm sorting out the ethics involved, you can read these.

CHAPTER 1

Introduction

✉

SUBJECT: Re: process printed labels, printed bags and packaging
TO: cascadeamerica
FROM: Jonathan Land <jland@incomplete.net>
DATE: 05/27/2003

WE PUT ALL THE PIECES TOGETHER

BUY DIRECT FROM THE MANUFACTURER

Cascade America can handle all your company's printing needs. We specialize in:

A. Diecut and printed labels

Spot printed with p.m.s color match up to 4 colors.

4 & 5 Color process printed labels.

- Print your labels in "vivid color" your image will jump right into view.

And now the easy part for pennies more than you are paying, you can upgrade your image by using distinctive, bright, crystal clear, photo-quality process printed labels; colorful, attractive, and very marketable. You can get full-color labels printed for little more than you are paying for your 1 and 2 color labels.

B. Package boxes, litho laminated boxes, gift boxes, gift packaging of all descriptions.

Cascade America is one of the nation's leading producers of form and fill packaging, using paper and film products. We use Flexographic and Rotogravure systems to print fine packages for industry.

C. Plastic Polybags for Apparel, Food Processors, and General industry.

At Cascade America, after 37 years in the printing industry, we have the knowledge and experience needed to produce the finest printed bags. Bags for industrial use in general and for the food industry in particular.

CASCADE AMERICA

Hello,

My name is Jonathan Land, and I have a bit of an odd request. I find myself saying that frequently, but I assure you that this time it's quite sincere. I'm not sure if a job like this is up your alley, but as they say, "He who doesn't attempt to try, tries to attempt to fail, and he too who tries twice to succeed, only succeeds twice in attempting to try to fail." That was written by the otherwise literate Frank Lloyd Wright after getting ridiculously drunk upon being informed of the second rejection of his first coffee-table book of architectural photos and sketches. Of course, as we all know, the third time was a charm for Mr. Wright, and multiple editions from countless publishers of his legendary coffee-table books can be found beneath every remote control in America.

I'm about to publish a coffee-table book of my own, entitled "The Spam Letters." It's a series of replies to unsolicited e-mail in a humorous vein. It's a joke book. I usually start off by making up some information about myself and what I require from the unwanted advertiser. Then I add some off-kilter but amusing detail, usually leading up to a series of bizarre statements (usually of a sexual nature, as that is what most spam is known for, and what an audience loves to read), wrapped in some requests that can be interpreted as being real. At the end I throw in some straightforward questions about the business at hand, in order to try to evoke a response. Of course, most of the e-mail addresses I reply to are dead, but on the rare occasions when I hear back and begin a correspondence, the humor is quite rewarding and is some of my best work. If I think I'm going to hit an address that responds, I try to keep my response low key; otherwise I go way over the top.

Anyhow, as goofy a concept as it is, this book means a lot to me, and I'm very concerned with my legacy, even though I know the material is flawed in terms of its having been created primarily to amuse myself. I consider this book to be my "masturpiece" -- it's THAT self-indulgent. Hey, that's a good one-liner. I should use it in one of The Letters.

For a coffee-table book that's going to be lying side by side with the work of a true genius like Frank Lloyd Wright, I have a whole lot to live up to. Frankly, I've been quite intimidated. So I've decided to part ways with my publisher, No Starch Press, and "fly solo" by entering the cold, cold world of self-publishing with my own finances to see to the printing of my own work. The one thing I've discovered so far in the publishing industry is that this business can be harder than, well, something unsavory I'd mention during a typical spam letter.

I've decided that what my book lacks in true artistic vision it will make up for in durability and heft. Every page will be laminated, and somehow weighed down. Thick, thick paper like a children's book, but it would need to be childproof, because of the content. Of course, if each page were too heavy for a child to lift, that would be a plus, but I guess that's a bit unrealistic.

"The Spam Letters" should be like a piano: the idea of owning it is rewarding somehow, but the burden of getting it into your home is so great that the thought of moving or otherwise disposing of it makes the owner shudder in horror long enough for the apathy to take hold.

I'm planning for an initial run of a modest 500 copies, and the book is about 250 pages long. After seeing your advertisement, I'm totally convinced that I'm better off using a specialty printing house that deals with lamination and thicker card stocks than using a traditional book manufacturer.

So (a) does this seem doable? And, most importantly, (b) how much will this cost?

Hopefully we can strike a deal since I'm doing a bulk thing here, and if the first run goes well (like Random House thought it would . . . that's why they signed me up before I began "becoming difficult"), there will be more.

I hope you're willing to work with me here, if you know what I'm saying,

Jonathan Land

CHAPTER 2

Products for Prey: Part 1

✉

You're ugly. You've lost your TV's remote . . . again. You're fat. You don't have enough gadgets. Your children need cooler toys. You can't perform in bed. If you can perform in bed, you can't do it well enough. Everyone you know is gossiping about these deficiencies and many, many more behind your back at this **VERY MOMENT.**

This chapter contains some of the more common (and frequent) spam solicitations I (and most likely you) have received. Simply hitting "delete" has never been satisfying enough for me.

✉

SUBJECT: Re: Hottest Gadget - Rc mini cars limited time
TO: Jean
FROM: Jonathan Land <jland@incomplete.net>
DATE: 11/20/2002

RC Mini Remote Controlled Race Cars - As seen on TV.

Sold out in stores. Best price in the country! First come first serve. Not
$39.95 or $29.95 Limited Time only $19.95ea. Hurry for Christmas

Race here Now

The all-new Mini RC Car is the latest craze for everyone of all ages! Each
Mini RC Car comes complete with remote control, mini car and carrying case.
It's a great gift for all ages. Take advantage of this special low price offer
today. Radio-frequency remote control - wireless! Super-Micro size receiver in
the car is less than 1" Has an independent front suspension Adjustable steer-
ing - Rubber tires Battery Charger Radio Controller included 5 Minutes Fast
Pace Action With Only 1 Minute of Charging Assembled and ready to race.

Hello, I've just gotten your e-mail, and I was wondering if your company
does any custom jobs. I run a charity, and the type of service you provide
would help me greatly with my work if you're able to think big. Here, let me
tell you the amusing tale of how my organization originated.

I was sitting outside a local supermarket in my Saturn, waiting for the crystal
meth to wear off a little so I wasn't so shaky and jumpy inside the store. It's
never good to look jumpy in a place of business, especially when the rent-
a-cops and store managers are just looking for some action to break up the
tedium. Did you know tedium is also an element on the periodic table? It
makes up 40% of the shell of a Saturn!

So I was just sitting there, popping some Valium, when a group of thuggish
high-school kids walked up to me and asked if they could bounce shopping
carts off my car. It seemed reasonable to me, highly entertaining for the
state I was in, and of little consequence to the tedium of my current state and
the durable mega-plastic crunchy outside of my vehicle, so I said, "Sure, go
for it."

Have you ever played the ancient video game Asteroids? That's what it
was like, except instead of turning, shooting, and dodging asteroids in my
spacecraft (it was more like a triangle), I was a sitting duck, observing all
the loose shopping carts in the parking lot barreling toward me, making

contact, then bouncing off as far as friction would let them go. And it was icy out, so man, did they go.

I felt like a proud and dexterous octopus father, playing catch with eight of my children simultaneously. It was a beautiful sight. It was like my own personal May Day, but instead of young, gleeful children dancing around with ribbons tethered to a large pole, despondent teens were actually having fun for once thanks to my tiny sacrifice, and my understanding that they needed to do this. It warmed my heart.

After a little while, I felt that I had reached a reasonable enough state to engage the shopping public. I kindly asked the kids to stop long enough for me to get out of the car. They did, and then they resumed the festivities. I thanked them, and told them if anyone starts hassling them to say that I'm in the store and that they are acting with my full permission.

As I headed toward the supermarket, I noticed that an employee had just finished waxing the floor. It was so shiny, and I pictured the shoppers inside gliding along with large strides, as if they were ice skating across the smooth linoleum.

Then it hit me. I turned around, got into the nearest shopping cart, and asked the nearest kid to do the honors. I sailed back to my car, made contact, recoiled a few inches, and then hopped out. I raised my hand in the air and everyone stopped. I gathered them around, and they seemed receptive to what I had to say.

"Listen. I don't want to give you a lecture here, but I hope you all realize that there's more to life than this. Things might seem bleak and dull to you right now, but believe me, I've been there. Things get better, trust me. You got to think bigger and do things beyond your expectations. Now everyone stand back, and I'll show you what I mean. Check this out."

I got into my car, started it up, did a few donuts in the parking lot to get up to speed, and then I drove directly toward the window of the supermarket where the large collection of shopping carts were parked. I got a nice lift off the sidewalk and plowed right through the glass, hitting the three tidy rows of carts at about 75 miles per hour.

They went ricocheting off in all directions, bouncing up and down the aisles, defying friction on the newly waxed floors. As the shoppers leapt forward and back depending on their position versus the oncoming carts, the wheels in motion were knocking stuff off the shelves from various sections, creating a reasonable but large collection of things to shop for in each cart. Like a hundred pinballs, they kept going through the store until the weight of the groceries forced them inevitably to stop. Nothing hit the ground, and not even the most sluggish octogenarian was hit.

The quick-thinking manager announced that anyone in the store who bought the contents of a given cart as is would get a 20% discount. I'm sure he realized, as I did, that it would save the staff the time and effort of restocking everything. And it worked! People perused the carts, found the one that best fit their needs, and proceeded to the checkout, where all the lanes were open and bustling. I think it's the first time I've ever seen that in any store.

There was a little fighting between shoppers over the carts that had occupants in the baby-seat portion of the cart. The parents of the toddler of a given cart felt that they were entitled to that particular cart, while other shoppers who were either considering having a baby or adopting, or were merely hearing their biological clock ticking off the seconds with a thunderous clap, snatched up the carts with the babies because they thought the kids would come with the discount.

Most of the babies were laughing, having just gone on their first thrill ride, except for one sissy in produce who was bawling and (I figure) crapped himself. For clarity, the manager then announced that all children would go home with the parents they originally arrived with.

I went over to the manager to apologize. I gave him my phone number and my address and asked him to send me the bill for the window I crashed through. He was a little peeved, but he realized that since people were buying the full shopping carts, the store was making a lot more money than usual. I then drove my car slowly through the automatic doors, with my flashers on, of course.

I stopped in front of the group of teens in the parking lot who were still in awe of my stunt. They all thought I was "the shit" (that's a good thing), and they seemed truly inspired.

"You see what I mean?" I said. "You've got to think big and believe in yourselves. But try not to cause too much property damage." I waved good-bye to them and went home.

The next day I got a call from the manager asking me to come over to the store. I got out my checkbook and went over to see him. When I got there, the window I'd broken had been replaced with sliding glass doors and a ramp up from the sidewalk. I walked in, and went over to the manager.

I apologized again and asked how much I owed him. For some reason he was smiling at me and giving me a look like he wanted to chase me around the salad bar and play grabass. He said, "Son, don't worry about it. It was our biggest non-holiday day ever!" I said, "Really? That's great. Are you sure you don't want me to pay for your new setup? I see that you took preventative measures with the ramp and sliding doors, but I promise to never do that again. I also had some youths looking on in admiration, but I already discussed the negative consequences about emulating my actions with them."

He cut me off. "Son, can you come here every Tuesday and pull off that stunt? I'm already having flyers made up for our 'Jackass Discount Tuesdays'."

"Really?"

"I swear on my dead mamma's mamma!"

"Sure!"

Well, wild and crazy guy that I am, I did that crowd-pleasing sales stunt every week after that for throngs of excited onlookers. I had my car painted with the name of the store, the amount of the discount, and the day and time of the event. In return, I got to fill up two shopping carts with my choice of delicacies, for free. Of course, since I did this every week, I had a stockpile of food well beyond what I could consume, so I became extremely popular with many charitable organizations that collect food and redistribute it to those in need. That felt really good.

I've since had several requests from other supermarkets to pull off the same stunt, and I'm happy to oblige. As of now, I'm pulling in 16 shopping carts full of groceries a week, and bombarding the charities with them.

Sure I'm pleased, but I see even greater potential here. I mean, why stop here? Why not take this program national? Imagine all the food donations! Of course, I'd promote my efforts with a cross-country road trip. I'd do my stuff with participating supermarkets along the way, who'd wax their floors to their shiniest for me. But obviously I can't be everywhere at once. I mean, I am just one person. I also would feel very uncomfortable having others attempting my potentially dangerous charity work because of the risk to self involved.

That's where you come in. I got your e-mail, and I started thinking that this might be a way to make this an even bigger show. I had the idea that you could rig a standard LS2 series Saturn to be remote-controlled with a larger-scale version of your RC Car remote-controlled receiver. Possibly even preprogram it with a timer to do its thing. Surely if scientists can launch unmanned rockets into space, you guys can launch an unmanned car up a ramp and through a window. Heck, you do it with little unmanned cars! Just think of how well this will reflect on your business! Don't make me have to team up with R.C. car conglomerate Radio Shack on this one. Let's keep this a grassroots thing.

So are you ready to think as big as I do? I can't tell you how rewarding this'll be.

Let me know if we can work together, and thanks,

Jonathan Land

SUBJECT: Re: Don't lose your remote cotrol again!
TO: 88NAQsp04
FROM: Jonathan Land <jland@incomplete.net>
DATE: 01/29/2003

THE ULTIMATE STAY-PUT REMOTE CONTROL KIT

Call (409) XXX-XXXX or (409) XXX-XXXX today!!

Are you tired of loosing the remote control to your TV, VCR, etc.?

Are you tired of looking for the remote and missing part of your favorite
program on the tube?

Have you been getting aggravated at the children, wife or husband because the
remote control won't stay put?

Maybe you just can't find it!

With the ULTIMATE STAY-PUT REMOTE CONTROL KIT, you may never have to look or
buy another remote control!! It can be yours for only $14.95!

The ULTIMATE STAY-PUT REMOTE CONTROL KIT, comes with your choice of a gold
or silver chain for the low price of only $14.95 (plus taxes and shipping
charges). During it's first promotional, the first 100 callers can receive 2
of the Stay-Put Remote Control Kit for only $19.99.

Remember, never loose your remote control again.

Call (409) XXX-XXXX or (409) XXX-XXXX today!!

Remove here. You must put your email address in the subject line or it will
not be removed: remoteoptout

Thank you

WOW! This is a brilliant idea!!!

I'm a prison guard in Jessup, MD, and when the inmates in my block get their
allotted TV time, they've taken to playing a new game that they refer to as
"Pass the Remote." The idea of the game is to swallow the TV's remote control and keep it in their digestive system for as long as possible. Everyone
gets a turn, and whoever takes the longest to "Pass the Remote" wins a pack
of cigarettes from everybody else.

Obviously the drug traffickers have the advantage in this type of situation. I mean, come on; these guys can swallow a balloon of cocaine and have it come out twisted into the shape of a schnauzer. Thing is, many drug traffickers have backgrounds as children's party clowns, but one toot of the horn leads to another, and clowning doesn't pay well, so the downward spiral into the life of crime begins. Anyway, these guys are good.

Hell, there's one guy who takes requests for channels and flips to them with intense bursts of well-directed flatulence. The guy's a genius. Of course, that only works once the remote has hit the lower GI tract. If it's not quite there yet, he just points me to the right place on his person, and I give him a little love tap with my billy club.

It's times like these when I feel like these creeps each have some kind of talent or a special gift they can give back to society, and they've just chosen the wrong path. YEAH, RIGHT!!! But hey, I'm not supposed to pass judgment, just enforce it with my mighty iron fist of whopping correctional power.

Anyhow, while all of this is highly entertaining, the remote controls get pretty foul pretty fast, so this whole thing needs to come to an end instead of in one and out the other. We've started replacing the remotes after every round of the contest, but we don't have much of a budget, and at the rate they're going, we won't be able to replace them past March. Then there's the whole unsanitary aspect. No one likes a lawsuit.

It would seem that your product could easily remedy this situation. I guess I just have two questions for you:

1) Do you accept purchase orders?

2) These are some bad dudes. Is the strength of the chain good enough so that they can't gnaw through it?

Please let me know.

I know this all might sound a bit odd, but this is actually pretty tame compared to some of the things I've seen, and your product would be a great service.

Jonathan Land

Corrections Officer, Block D3

Jessup, MD

SUBJECT: Re: At Last, Herbal V, the All Natural Alternative is Available!
TO: HV
FROM: Jonathan Land <jland@incomplete.net>
DATE: 2/02/2002

Herbal V: An Incredible All-Natural Healthy Alternative To V----a

Herbal V is the All Natural Approach to Male Virility, Vitality and Pleasure.

Available N o w !

Welcome to the New Sexual Revolution.

It's the all natural male potency and pleasure pill that men everywhere are
buzzing about. Herbal V is safe, natural and specifically formulated to help
support male sexual function and pleasure. You just take two easy-to-swallow
tablets one hour before sex. And there's more great news - you can get Herbal
V for less than $1 a pill.

Amazing word of mouth praise on Herbal V has been spreading like wildfire-
already over 1,500,000 men have chosen Herbal V. Since it is 100% natural you
will never have to worry about safety. Try doctor-recommended Herbal V today
and have the greatest night of your life!

Herbal V... Bringing Back the Magic!

Boy, do I have a bone to pick with you.

You should really pay more attention to who you send your advertising to.
I am a 17-year-old college student, who, as any average 17-year-old male
could tell you, is sexually excited more often than not. If a butterfly flaps its
wings in China, I guarantee you there isn't an atomic clock that can accu-
rately measure the speed with which I will pitch a tent.

I know you were hoping to get some 45-year-old dentist who has spent the
past 20 years of his life with a woman who makes any given NPR personal-
ity look like a sex kitten, and yes, that includes the guys from "Car Talk."
My point is this: because of your primitive "marketing strategy," you have
screwed me over BIG TIME!

I've been seeing this girl for about three months now, and I've finally figured out the right combination of sensitivity and alcohol to coerce her into
relieving me of that mighty, mighty albatross: virginity. So, we're back at my
room in the frat house. We start making out a little and I need to go to the
bathroom because I'm wicked blitzed, and I haven't taken a leak all night. So

she asks, "While you're gone, do you mind if I download some mood music off of Napster?" Since I only have Limp Bizkit CDs, I have no "sensitive, love-making music," so I say, "Sure, get some Smashing Pumpkins or shit like that, Baby." Am I good or what?

So I'm in the bathroom thinking: Okay, if I take her clothes off at the rate of one article every 10 minutes (an efficient, yet sensitive pace -- I'm a math major), I will be losing my virginity within the hour, but then I realize: Hey, we're in Buffalo, NY. In winter. Who knows how many layers of clothing she's wearing! I might stay a virgin for two more hours! I can't take it! (That's when I remembered that I had my thermal underwear on, and that just ain't manly by any yardstick, so I got rid of them.)

I come out of the bathroom, and she's just sitting there with this completely different expression on her face. She says: "Sweetie, I saw that e-mail about the natural Viagra stuff that your friend sent you. It's okay, we don't need to rush this." I was completely torn. I can't say something like, "Yo, that ain't true, I'll make sweet, sweet love to you senseless right here, right now, over and over and over" without giving up the sensitive front. So I say, "Baby, I'm sorry you had to find out about my erectile dysfunction this way, but I'd like to try this. I'd like to try and make you happy." She was on board. Kid Genius had saved the day!

So we were fooling around for a few hours, and all I'm thinking from the get-go is: "Okay, why am I not hard yet?" This girl is a cheerleader for Christ's sake, and my penis is acting like I'm in bed with Nathan Lane. After a while she gets real frustrated, calls me a fag, goes home, and the next day she's doing one of my fraternity brothers. My one prospect of virginity-loss has slipped through my hands like a grain of sand in an hourglass, a moment in time that cannot be regained, just like that grain of sand that will never pass through the glass chamber in the same way, no matter how many times you flip the thing over. And believe me, I tried flipping her over, and that didn't work either. (I've got a minor in philosophy -- can you tell??)

Did you know that some ancient tribes from South America, such as the Yanomamo, punish murderers not only for the people they've killed, but for the deaths of the potential descendants of those people as well? Well I should fucking sue you to the tune of all the girls I could have done by now if I lost my virginity as scheduled. All because of you, I'm still a virgin. Maybe since last week I could have banged 30 chicks a night, but I'll never know now. I'm just sitting around waiting for the mayor of Poonville to award me the medal of pity and give me the key to the city.

Thanks loads, dude,

Jon

SUBJECT: Re: Open Any Lock with Kwick Pick - On Sale Today!
TO: Kwick Pick
FROM: Jonathan Land <jland@incomplete.net>
DATE: 05/29/2003

NEVER PAY FOR A LOCKSMITH AGAIN!

Open almost any lock with Kwick Pick. This versatile and lightweight portable lock pick can open padlocks, car doors, file cabinets, front door locks, desk drawers, toolboxes, luggage, gas caps, and much more.

Never Pay for a Locksmith Again! This locksmith-in-a-pocket weighs just over an ounce. It fits comfortably in your hand, and opens practically any lock. Kwick Pick comes in especially handy when you've locked your keys in the car, or in the house. Buy one for yourself, or as a gift.

I've already put in an order for your excellent product, but I'm curious about what other items you have to offer in terms of surveillance, weapons, and explosives. I'm trying to prepare for a bank heist with a few co-conspirators, and being able to get our collective foot in the door . . . literally . . . while the bank's closed is a major coup. So thank you for that, but to not come off like the rank amateurs we really are, we'll need to prepare for what awaits us in terms of bank security after that.

Just so you know, we're going to hit the Shovelers and Plowers Credit Union in West Fargo, North Dakota, on 18th and Devine. Casing the place will be difficult, since the entire town is familiar with everyone on my team, so we'll have to make an educated guess about what's inside and what type of vault it is.

My name's Jonathan Land. I'm involved strictly as an organizer, because if one of the tellers sees me, she'll know something's up. I've already assembled an excellent team of wannabe burglars to assist me in my cause. I think we can do this as a team of ten, but we have one extra random guy tacked on to prove that we can go one better than that!

Here's the plan:

Once we get in the door, there are probably going to be motion sensors. Billy "PseudoSpiderman" Peters will climb up the walls and across the ceiling, out of range of the detectors to disable them. He can do this, thanks to his custom-made suit of duct tape, Velcro, and actual cobwebs he's collected from his very own attic.

Once the sensors are disabled, we'll get down to the basement where there better be some of those infrared laser beams that trigger alarms when you break the beam. If there aren't, I'll be sorely disappointed, because they look so cool in the movies. For this hurdle we have "Limber" Larry Loveowski, who works as a limbo contest shark on cruise lines and island resorts. There's no contest he can't win, and no one stoops as low as him -- I mean that with the utmost respect. He'll get under those beams, no problem.

Now, Larry can bend at the shins, but there's still the possibility that some lasers could be below that, so we have Arnold "The Levitator" Schwartz to give Larry a psycho-kinetic boost should it be necessary. I've never seen him move stuff with his mind, but he tells me he's been practicing. He said he lifted a wallet from a guy once, and he claims to have gotten a girl "real high" at a Phish show.

So now we're at the safe, and this is when The Mighty 'Mite Twins come into play. While he's never personally toyed with explosives, we've got Jimmy "J.J." Walker on the team, and he is self-proclaimed DY-NO-MIIIIIITE. Then we've got Rudy Ray Moore, who's Dolemite. His explosive brand of put-down humor will tear stuff up and blow you away. The man's got as many guns as he does women.

While the aforementioned are carrying out the technical details of the crime, we'll need a couple of distractions in case anyone's hanging out outside the bank, or if we don't get to this part before the bank reopens the following day.

"Kaiser" Jose Hernandez can fake any physical illness, though sometimes he switches in midstream. One time he was establishing a front as a quadriplegic with MS, and one day he showed up as a "mentally challenged" guy just dragging the left side of his body like he had cerebral palsy. He covered for that one somehow by saying he got "a little cured," but he did do jail time when his "amputated arm" kept switching sides while trying to collect disability from the government. Jose's good when he can focus, though. He can even do jaundice and sunburn on the spot. The guy's a chameleon. Anyway, for our purposes he might just fake a seizure or something, and shriek loudly so J.J. and Rudy Ray can do their thing.

Once we've got the cash, we'll run like the wind out the back door and let our escape crew have their time to shine. Frankie "The Choker" Charles will suck down a carton of cigarettes and puff out a wall of smoke so dense that anyone who dares try to get through his "chain smoke fence" will be spitting out tumors for the rest of their truncated life.

Our getaway driver is Double Drag'n, a drag-racing drag queen who's been forced into learning how to drive like hell since he/she grew up in an intolerant community. The only thing worse than being beaten by a girl from the perspective of a drag-racing teenager is being beaten by a guy in drag.

After we empty out the vault, we'll leave this note:

> You don't know me, but if you want your money back, one of your tellers (Becky) better give Jon Land his ABBA CD, some naked photos of herself, and a little respect and dignity. Or maybe you should just give him a call or something.
>
> - a concerned friend of Jon Land that doesn't know him at all.

If all of that doesn't make her realize that she's wronged me, then she's an idiot who doesn't deserve a go-getting happening guy like me!!! (I know I come off as a hard kind of guy, but I really love her, and I think this'll win her back.)

Anyway, as you see, there's a lot of involved details, so if you have anything that might help us execute any of the above, please let me know, because I'll be your best customer. And you can take that to the bank . . . YOU KNOW I WILL!!! HAHAHAHAHAHA!

Oh, and pretty please, don't use any of this information against us if you're not going to hook us up. That just wouldn't be cool. Thanks!

Jonathan Land

on behalf of Land's Eleven (Minus Two)

✉

SUBJECT: Re: Take Pringles' Spicy Quiz!
TO: yahoo-delivers
FROM: Jonathan Land <jland@incomplete.net>
DATE: 03/03/2003

Take Pringles' "How Spicy are You?" Quiz So do you think you're pretty spicy? Find out just how spicy you really are!

Take our "How Spicy are You?" quiz. A unique quiz that plays like a game and reveals your truly spicy nature. To take the quiz, go here:

http://[URL deleted]

Our quiz isn't the only hot news! You see, things are really heating up at Pringles! We're talking serious flavor! Hot and fiery, spicy, peppery flavor! New Spicy Cajun Pringles are irresistible.

Now you're one of the first to know about Spicy Cajun Pringles and our "How Spicy are You?" quiz.

http://[URL deleted]

> Listen, my girlfriend is a Latina woman, and she just took your "How Spicy Are You?" quiz, and she ranked "Hot and Bothered," which is the second category from the bottom.
>
> I don't know if you're aware of this, but Latina women pride themselves in being "Hot and Spicy," and "Hot Tamales," and "Spicy-a Meat-a-balls," and all that, so needless to say, she's quite upset that your test is claiming that she's not as hot as she's accustomed to being.
>
> I was trying to comfort her by saying that the whole quiz was timed, and that she doesn't do well in high-pressure situations. Plus, she was never good at standardized tests to begin with. Unfortunately, she's still down. Pouting might be considered attractive to a few, but it is not necessarily hot, or spicy. I'd like to encourage her to take the test again, but in this state, she'll be lucky to get "tepid and bland." My little jalapeno is turning to tofu-flavored jelly before my very eyes.
>
> I have a simple request: Can you PLEASE put a version of the quiz up that will display the "Hot and Spicy" result every time? Would that be difficult to do? I've been a big fan of your product for years, and I can back that claim up with all of my grocery store receipts. I'll be sure to buy a tube of the new flavor and swear by it in front of all the popular local supermarkets. Please?
>
> Thank you,
>
> Jonathan Land

✉

SUBJECT: Re: Cheap Cigarettes Online
TO: kamie009
FROM: Jonathan Land <jland@incomplete.net>
DATE: 02/05/2003

Cheap Cigarettes on Line

Did you know you could buy cigarettes CHEAP on the Internet?

We have 39 styles of cigarettes priced @ $9.99 a carton.

MarlboroÃs @ $26.10, Generics @ $23.40.

Visit our website:

http://[URL deleted]

Excuse me Sir/Madam,

Do you sell marijuana cigarettes? In case you're worried, I have not been a child or a narcotics officer for many years, and I have cataracts you can pick out with a fork. I need this real bad.

I'm sorry, did I say cataracts? I meant glaucoma. Now point me to a secret backdoor portion of your site where I can lawfully obtain marijuana cigarettes!

Det. Jonathan Land (Ret.)

SUBJECT: Re: Save on Shipping Tape...Stretch Film...Bubble
TO: TigerTape, Inc
FROM: Jonathan Land <jland@incomplete.net>
DATE: 05/27/2003

ATTN: PURCHASING CALL: 1-800-XXX-XXXX››››

We are master distributors of a complete line of packaging tapes. Our marketing strategy is to sell our products directly to the end user of shipping tapes. We also offer industrial tapes such as duct, electrical, filament, teflon, stationery tapes, poly strapping tapes, custom printed tapes etc., as well as hard to find specialty tapes. The tape we are offering below is 1.9 mils. thick, and has an acrylic adhesive that works well in all temperature ranges. This tape exceeds postal requirements and works well sealing boxes with contents weighing up to 200 pounds.›

Let us give you a qoute on stretch film/pallet wrap ˜.. we operate on a very low margin of profit so TigerTape is able to offer YOU the customer, the very best prices available ! ››› 2" X 110 yard carton sealing tape››››››››››››› $ .99 per roll

Clear or Brown/ 36 rolls per case--- ›› Stretch Film (Pallet Wrap) Savings/
Call for Pricing ››› " X 60 yard Nylon filament strapping tape $ .99 per roll

48 rolls per case

3" X 700 foot 120 gauge Stretch Film › $2.49 per roll

18 rolls per case

>>> COMPLETE LINE OF RAINWEAR¯..RAINSUITS,PONCHOS,JACKETS,RAINCOATS <<<

FREIGHT PAID on 3 cases ANYWHERE in the Continental U.S.

CALL FOR PALLET PRICING

Contact us at: 1 - 800 - XXX - XXXX

Lee Warren

TigerTape, Inc

If you wish to be removed from our list, please respond with "REMOVE" typed
in your subject line.› We always honor all removal requests.... Thank you for
your time.

What's your most soundproof tape?

My business associates and I own and operate a wire hanger factory in New
Jersey, and sometimes we deal with equipment that gets a little noisy and
needs some quieting down. So we use the tape to stop the equipment from
squealing until we can properly determine if it needs replacing or an over-
haul, if you know what I'm saying.

Currently we have a lot of equipment that we've recently acquired from a
former competitor that needs to be dealt with, and we have some questions as to where said equipment's loyalties lie. Some of the equipment isn't
performing as expected, what with the squealing and all. All that squealing
draws some unwanted attention to the factory, and we don't like attention.

So we see ourselves buying in bulk, as we have many issues to deal with in
regards to the problems I've laid out above.

If you could let me know what your most soundproof tape is, I'd be much
obliged, and would then proceed to do a little business with you and yours.

Vincent Garibaldi

Manager of Imports and Exports

Giustefrant Hangers

SUBJECT: Re: Natural Viagra 12154
TO: joke79
FROM: Jonathan Land <jland@incomplete.net>
DATE: 06/04/2003

Alternative to Viagra!

Click Here to Spice Up Your Sex Life Today!

Do you want to improve your Sex Life?

IMPULSE is an all Natural Herbal formula that is guaranteed to increase your sexual performance! Remember, it's all natural so your body doesn't get harmful side effects.

IMPULSE HERBAL BENEFITS:

1. Gives Long-Lasting and Powerful Erections!

2. You Don't Need a Prescription to buy IMPULSE!

3. Very Affordable PRICE! (1/10 the cost of Viagra!)

4. Revitalizes the sex interest in both partners

5. Sex plays a vital part in any relationship! Bring back that missing piece!

6. Never Any Negative Side Effects! (All Natural Ingredients)

7. Helps women with a sexual response dysfunction

Ordering is very simple and completely anonymous. You don't have to wait another day to improve your sex life, you now have an all natural solution!

The #1 best selling 100% all natural aphrodisiac in America!

Increase Your Sex Life Today! IMPULSE!

To be taken off send email to here

. . . .

Ha ha ha, he he he, and ho ho ho to you my useless friend.

I've realized something lately: You people who send out these e-mails aren't targeting them specifically at me! I'm not being plagued by rumors of sexual incompetence. The brothers in the frat house aren't playing a demoralizing prank at my expense (for once). They're just random!

My first run-in with a "Natural Viagra" spam took place last December as I was trying desperately to lose my virginity. That day I lost my wallet, my car keys, most of my ambition, and my grandma, so there was definitely something magical afoot in regards to the physical and emotional sensations of loss. I had this totally hot cheerleader in my room, and we were about to do the nasty for the first time (for me at least; she's been around) when that ad popped up. She read it, questioned my sexual prowess, and then bolted, misinterpreting my ensuing performance anxiety for a more serious sexual dysfunction that can only be aided by tools from the medical establishment meant for much older men. I was bummed, man . . . she was a cheerleader!!! I just sat there afterward wondering how . . . how could someone fuck me over by sending me such a thing? I vowed then and there to immediately throw out every bit of junk mail I'd ever receive.

My second run-in with a "Natural Viagra" spam happened last week. Being confined to the cold prison of self-love since December, I turned myself to other callings besides trying to score with the babes. I immersed myself in my studies. I didn't even know I had studies until Coach told me. If I'm sending you this e-mail: Thanks Coach!

I thought . . . I'm going to break myself out of the stereotype of the dumb jock . . . and the love will follow. Well, it turns out that not only am I dumb enough to be assigned tutors in four subjects, but I'm not that good of a jock either. I've been warming the bench for the past 15 games. I guess at 6' 5" and 130 pounds I shouldn't be playing football anyway. My nickname's "The Javelin." I can't get ahead of myself though. I'll pump up my body after I pump up my mind. WOOFWOOFWOOF!!!

The task is daunting, but still I forge on. I was studying applications of kinematics with my physics tutor when said second "Natural Viagra" message popped up on my computer as she was looking for a good online reference for standard formulae. I saw it, and I was like, "Move it or lose it, dork chick." I darted in front of her to dismiss the message ASAP. I have a reputation to protect, even amongst the people who might not be aware of the rep to begin with.

But it was too late. She saw it and was like, "Did that say 'Natural Viagra?'" and I was like, "Uh, no . . . it said 'Natural Niagara.' I love that place; they sell the fragrance in an aerosol can. It's just like being there." Quick thinking, huh??? Am I good or what?

Then she started saying all this weird cryptic stuff. She was like, "Oh, well, you must have already sprayed some in here because I'm getting all misty and wet." And I was like, "Huh? No I haven't really gotten it yet, that was just an order confirmation," and then she took off those ridiculously oversized glasses that she wears and put them on the desk.

So then she was like, "You know, if you want to cross the border, you can explore my duty-free shop." I was like, "Huh? What the fuck are you talking about?" And then she took that thingy out of her tightly wrapped bun and shook her head, allowing her surprisingly long hair to fall wildly around her.

At this point, I wasn't even sure why she was still trying to talk about Niagara Falls when I had a physics quiz the next day . . . but she went on. She was like, "If I were Niagara Falls, I'd like you to get in a barrel and go down on me." I was like, "I thought you could get arrested for doing that; don't they have Mounties stopping people from doing that?" By the time she said, "Ooh, let's play Mounties," and she was bopping up and down and clapping her hands like a retard, I had had enough of this, but for some reason she was topless, and I was like, "Holy shit . . . those are breasts!"

Then she said the first thing I understood in about 45 minutes: "Let's have sex." And I was like, "Now you're talkin'." Chicks are so confusing. Why couldn't she have said that a whole lot earlier? I learned a lot about kinetic frictional force that night. Not necessarily "book" friction, but "street" friction. It's a lesson I paid close attention to, and it has solidly convinced me that learning is fun. I might have failed the quiz, but I passed a milestone of life.

Yes, I lost my virginity that night. Thanks to this very e-mail. However, I won't be needing your product. I can handle things just fine. I'm still upset that I get these e-mails from you and your kind that wreak havoc on my life, but this time it's actually worked to my benefit. It's a mixed blessing though, and to give you some satisfaction that my life isn't now the post-virginal ideal, I will mention this:

It's customary to brag/gloat amongst my people after the acquisition of a new sexual experience, whether it's the 1st or the 10,000th, but there are certain mitigating factors that could possibly deter one from taking part in the traditional festivities. Yes, I had sex, but it was with a dork chick. A nerd, a geek . . . one of them . . . and so while I am no longer a virgin . . . no one must know, and for that I am ashamed.

Now if you could only make a pill that will make my new dork sex chick socially acceptable to my brothers in the frat house that I can discreetly dump in the water supply . . . then I'd be impressed. I'd also be your first customer.

Jon

SUBJECT: Re: Sexual Enhancement & FREE Herbs!
TO: gordon
FROM: Jonathan Land <jland@incomplete.net>
DATE: 07/03/2003

Greetings & Blessings To You!

Offering for your "Sensitive" Delight:

1. "Seventh Heaven" Kathmandu Temple Kiff (tm); a viripotent cannabis alternative for blissful regressions of vexatious depressions...

2. Sweet Vjestika Aphrodisia Drops (tm); An erotic aphrodisia; sexual intensifier / enhancer liquid amalgamated extract for MEN and WOMEN.

3. "Seventh Heaven" Prosaka Tablets (tm); a botanical alternative to pharmaceutical medications for calm, balance, serenity and joyful living...

4. "Seventh Heaven" Gentle Ferocity Tablets (tm); a most efficacious, non-caffeine, non-ephedrine, non-MaHuang botanical energizer and cutting-edge appetite suppressant...

Coolness!

I'm currently working on my own natural alternatives to prescription drugs! Maybe we can hook up and sell our stuff over the Net together.

Here's what I have to offer:

"Valley Yum" -- Bubble gum for when you need to come down off of that peak. "Valley Yum" is made from super-concentrated turkey, turkey broth, and rib meat. You'll give thanks when you can sleep easy and through the night!

"AZTea" -- A minty beverage that'll boost any compromised immune system with 10,000,000% of the daily allowance of Vitamin C (but not the kind of "Vitamin C" we sell -- "C" below).

"Long Island AZTea" -- The cocktail version of "AZTea," which features vodka and rum . . . not for sale to anyone who can't fake not being a minor.

"Vitamin C" -- This is actually Codeine, but since it's cleverly mislabeled, no legal authority would dare closely inspect this product unless you're cross-ing a border with it. This is our biggest seller.

"Placebo Domingo" -- These zesty, tangy pills will cure whatever ails you! These pills are so powerful, we've discretely packaged them as Pez, also in the hopes of avoiding legal scrutiny.

"RU Nuts" -- A breakfast cereal that's so yummy and nutritious, it's great for every morning after! "RU Nuts" is made from only the finest 18th century herbal ingredients that'll rock your world! Warning -- "RU Nuts" contains almonds.

Whadda think?

Jon

✉

Author's Note: Spam donated by Hélène de Grosbois.

SUBJECT: Re: BURN-OFF BODY FAT QUICK AND EASY!
TO: instant_results_guaranteed
FROM: Jonathan Land <jland@incomplete.net>
DATE: 08/20/2003

Burn-off Those Pounds Fast!

~STAY THIN FOR LIFE~ You can Look your Best Now!

Get the Stay-N-Thin Rapid Burn Diet NOW!! StayThin is an Extra Strength Herbal Diet Supplement NEW BREAKTHROUGH FAT BURNING FORMULA

Click here to learn more:

Now you can burn fat, faster than you ever thought possible. Not only for weight loss ! See what else this cutting edge formula helps you with:

• Burn off body fat quickly and easily

• Have more energy

• Suppress your appetite

• Elevate your mood

• Boost your immune system

- Reduced water retention

- Fight free radical damage with potent antioxidants

- Feel better overall

Lose up to 30 lbs in 29 days "Results Guaranteed"

It is not too late to look great with this Diet.

Click here to learn more:

This is the Fastest and easiest way to lose weight Safely...

Dear Charlatan,

I don't believe your "diet" actually works. It's inherently flawed. It requires people to consume a "supplement." Helloooooo!!!! The whole idea of a diet is to REDUCE yourself . . . not INCREASE. Duh.

I have a diet too. One that works. I call it the Jon Land Lucky Seven Point Diet, and you don't need to take anything for it.

1. Go to your local cut-rate Wal-Mart and buy an exercise device that's as close to $30 as you can find, and assemble it.

2. If you consume as much soda as I do, consume half that amount. If you don't consume soda at all, then there's no way you can lose weight, and you should learn to grow comfortable with your current sense of self.

3. Turn your air conditioner off in the summer. Sweat is liquid fat.

4. Cut your hair and clip your toenails. Every bit counts.

5. Balance your feet at the "sweet spots" of your scale, usually near the extreme edges, where the reading is at the lowest . . . anything above that number is a "bonus pound" that isn't worth mentioning.

6. Flip your mattress; that has to burn calories. If your mattress is less than queen sized, flip it with someone on it, and then hang on tight while they struggle free. If they don't struggle free, carry (don't drag) the body to your car, drive it out to the country, and throw it in a large river. This is GREAT exercise; you probably won't have to exercise again for another month.

7. Evacuate early, evacuate often. Remember: When you've got to go on a scale of one to two, aim high.

Your diet is a total joke. When I get around to marketing mine, you better watch out. There's a lean, mean kid in town, and I'll snatch away all of your customers that you're plumping up like veal.

Jonathan Land

CHAPTER 3
Foreign Affairs: Part 1

〰〰〰〰〰〰〰〰〰〰〰〰〰〰〰〰〰 ✉ 〰〰〰〰〰〰〰〰〰〰〰〰〰〰〰〰〰

I'm not the type of person who likes to take advantage of others . . . unless they're attempting to take advantage of me. That's when the gloves come off, which is just as well since typing in gloves is difficult, mittens even more so.

These letters contain correspondence from people in India and Pakistan's textile industry. Why they would send out mass e-mails for such a specific service is beyond me, but that's the "beauty" of e-mail. These folks didn't seem to be malicious spammers, but this material seemed appropriate to spin a few yarns with.

〰〰〰〰〰〰〰〰〰〰〰〰〰〰〰〰〰 ✉ 〰〰〰〰〰〰〰〰〰〰〰〰〰〰〰〰〰

MY BUDDY KUTTY

....

SUBJECT: Re: trade enquiry
TO: abiramii abiramii
FROM: Jonathan Land <jland@incomplete.net>
DATE: 10/10/2000

TO THE IMPORTING MANAGER

HELLO

ONE OF QUALITY EXPORTER OF HIGH FASHIONED KNITTED GAEMENTS IN INDIA. WE HAVE WE WOULD LIKE TO INTRODUCE OURSELF AS 10 YEARS EXPERIENCE IN THIS BUSSINESS. OUR EXPERIENCE IS BASED UPON SOUND UNDERSTANDING OF THE MANUFACTURING PROCESS AND AN INOVATION APPROACH TO FULFILL YOUR NEEDS. OUR PRODUCT WILL APPEAL TO EVERYONE WHO DESIRES THE BEST COMBINATION OF COST QUALITY & STYLE.

WE USE FABRIC SUCH AS SINGEL JERSEY ,PIQUE, INTERLOCK, JACQUARD,DROP NEEDLE, LOOPKNIT, YARN-DYED ETC. USING 100% COTTON MELANGE,BLENDED ,POLYESTER&LYCRA YARNS.OUR WIDE AND VARIED RANGE OF CASUAL & ACTIVEWEAR INCLUDE TÚSHIRTS POLOSHIRTS, SWEATSHIRTS, NIGHT DRESSES,SHIRTS, BLOUSES, CO-ORDINATES, TANK TOPS, SKIRTS, SHORTS, JOG SUITS BODYSUITS, JUMP SUITS, PANTS ,LEGGINGS, SWEAT-ERS ,CARDIGANS, BESIDES IN ALL STYLE AND SIZE RANGE. WE ARE THE ONE OF THE STOCKIST OF STOCK DYEDYARNS. WE CAN GIVE CHEAPEST PRICE OF YARN DYED STRIPES POLO SHIRTS USING STOCK DYED YARNS. WHATEVER YOUR STRIPES DESIGH COLOUR COMB AND FABRIC WE CAN MAKE IT. WE ARE MAKING ECO-FRIENDLY CARRY BAG IN KNITTED IN VERY LOW PRICE.

YOU CAN CONTACT US THROUGH FAX +91-421-XXXXXX & NET(abiramii@) at your office time itself.

OUR COMMUNIOCATION ADDRESS.

ABIRAMII FASHIONS,

EXPECTING YOUR FAVOURABLE REPLY

SINCERELY

KUTTY.S

Hello!

My name is Jonathan Land, the Importing Manager for Incomplete Industries. The sweatshop I currently manufacture my merchandise in is under intense government scrutiny, so your mailing has come just in time!

We sell "brand-name" replicas of famous name items (Hilfiger, Fubu, Lauren, Stewart) as well as merchandise with replicas of cultural icons (Mickey Mouse, Simpsons, O.J., Rodney King) to the inner-city market at a fraction of what it would cost our clients to purchase a firearm or the legitimate versions of these products. It's our way of giving back to the community AND making a buck.

So what are your rates, and what's your turnover time?

Looking forward to working with you!

Jonathan Land

Importing Manager, Incomplete Industries

✉

*Author's Note: T-shirt designers include **Jeff Hobbs** and **Joshua Newman**.*

....

SUBJECT: Re: SAMPLES ATTACHMENTS; i
TO: abiramii abiramii
FROM: Jonathan Land <jland@incomplete.net>
DATE: 10/14/2000

DEAR JONATHAN LAND, HOW ARE YOU

.THANKS FOR YOUR REPLY.PLEASE NOTE WE SENT SOME ATTACHED FILES OF MY SAMPLES. YOU SELECT AND GIVE ME YOUR FAVOURABLE REPLY THEN WE CAN GIVE OUR RATES AND TURNOVER TIME

THANKS&REGARDS

S.KUTTY

Hello,

Sorry for the delay, I literally had my nose in a vice. Yowsers! Note to myself: Don't bounce a check on the mafia! Know what I mean? I had the money; it just wasn't in the right account.

Anyhow, I've had my designers enclose designs within the style parameters you sent me in your mailings. Some notes:

-All items with lettering must be that puffy, fuzzy sort of iron-on style lettering. What fonts to you have for that?

-For the adult men's and women's clothing, PLEASE make sure that there's a little extra room in the seat/crotch of the pants. My experience in the inner-city clothing industry has taught me one thing: Know your customers. My customers are oblong-pear shaped, if you know what I mean. This must be taken into account. My clients DO NOT appreciate snugly fitting clothes. I realize this is only a precaution since most of the men wear their pants absurdly low, but that's what being a good businessman is all about, and I am respected in the community as a businessman.

Here are the quantities I'll need:

Image 1: 10

Image 5: 25

Image 3: 5

Image 9: 50 (This design's our biggest seller!)

Image 2: 10

Image 6: 25

Image 4: 30 each

Image 8: 25

Image 7: 10

So let's get down to brass tacks: How much, and when my good man? The ball's (I just said "balls"! ha ha!) in your court! We are ready to roll here!

Jon

welcome to our "pol"!
notice there is
no second "o"
it, please keep
it that way

If you're able
to read this
you're not
squeezing
my boobs yet

n.a.m.b.l.a-rama !!

21 cents an
hour...
and all I made
was this lousy
T-shirt!

i'm a strain
on daddy's
finances

SUBJECT: Re: re-enquiry- ii
TO: abiramii abiramii
FROM: Jonathan Land <jland@incomplete.net>
DATE: 10/18/2000

DEAR JON

WE RECEIVED YOUR MAIL. WE HERE YOUR REQUIREMENT. WE CAN MAKE SAMPLES ASAP.
PLEASE SEND YOUR MEASUREMENT SPEC& PRINTING POSITIONS AND COLOUR SOURCE AND
FABRIC RANGE.

> Whoa, there buddy! Hold your horses. Maybe we should discuss money
> before you go through the effort of making samples.

THEN ONLY WE CAN WORK.PLEASE SEND IMMEDIATLY. PLEASE NOTE WE CAN RECEIVED YOUR
PAYMENT ONLY ON TELAX TRASFER OR DEMAND DRAFT.

> Sweet Jesus! Or Sacred Cow! You already received payment? Who did you
> speak to in Accounts Payable? I know nothing about this; I haven't approved
> anything yet. Are you going over my head here? I thought we had a reason-
> able relationship. Did you talk to Joshua? That dummy ruins everything! I
> almost had a new assistant last week who could hook me up with one of
> those Thailand mail-order brides, but Joshua scared him off. After I send out
> this e-mail, I'm going to fire him. What's going on here?

I SEND BALLS IN YOUR COURT(I JUST SAID "BALLS" HA HA HA!)

> Good one! I like dealing with people who have good heads on their shoul-
> ders and an excellent sense of humor, and until now I've held you in the
> highest regard. Don't mess with me at this stage in the game.
>
> Jon

*Author's Note: I can't tell if Mr. Kutty is calling me "Joe" here as an affectionate
nickname, or if he responds to his mail under the effect of sweet Asian opiates.*

SUBJECT: Re: SAMPLES ATTACHMENTS; i
TO: abiramii abiramii
FROM: Jonathan Land <jland@incomplete.net>
DATE: 12/12/2000

dear joe how are you.iam fine.i like to know ifyou buy stocklots.

It's been too long, Mr. Kutty. I hope things are going well for you. And yes, we deal with stocklots.

because my client goods have cancelled in your country. the stock details below

The merchandise is okay, though, right? I don't want damaged goods. No sir, if I wanted that, I would have voted this year. Have you heard what's been going on here in the U.S., or does your government censor (or at the very least delay) the news? The censors will probably edit this next part out, but here goes nothing: America is in a very weak state right now. If your government wants to take a run at some sort of military operation against us, now is the time. This country is ripe for the plucking, and the citizens definitely think it's time for something new. I'd be more than happy to help as your man on the inside. Just between you and me, though, does the caste system really work? Would it work here?

THE STOCK DETAILS

LABEL; STAFFORD

TAG; JC PENNY

MENS BRIEF ; 39066 PCS

MENS BOXER SHORTS ;44,674 PCS

MENS V-NECK T-SHIRT;46,004 PCS

SIZE;M,L,XL,XXL,XXXL

How much for the whole thing, and also how much for just the XXLs and XXXLs? As I've mentioned previously, our customers are big from the waist down. My clients have to smoke nothing but . . . what do they call it . . . I think it's called crack-cocaine. Yeah, that's right, nothing but crack-cocaine for a month to fit into the smaller sizes, but one of my partners is trying to think of another way we can use these things. We might be able to market them as hats as long as we throw them onto a few of our well-planted "cool kids" that we put out on the street to infiltrate the community and establish trends.

FABRIC;SINGLE JERSY LYCRA5%

GSM; 180

COLOUR; BLACK,WHITE,NAVY, CHARCOAL

CTN PER PCS;48PCS

WE GLAD TO INFORM THE GOODS IS IN A AMERICAN PORT. LATE SHIPMENT IS THE CANCEL STORY

Where's the port? East coast or west? This will be a big factor in terms of shipping.

TODAY OR TOMMOROW I CAN GIVE A PICTURE IN MAIL. IF YOU LIKE TO SEE THE SAMPLE PLEASE ADVISE YOUR COURIER ACCOUND NUMBER.

The pictures look darn good, but I have two requests:

1) Is it too late for you to print logos or text on the merchandise?

2) Can you spray the clothing thoroughly with a chemical compound I'll send you? This compound speeds up the deterioration of most fabrics, so something made out of cotton (for example) will last only a third as long as its unsprayed counterpart, and it'll last a third of THAT amount if the garment in question is ever washed, which could happen. It ensures repeat business, and a lot of U.S. manufacturers are doing it these days.

Answer these questions please, so I have a better idea of what the situation is.

Thanks,

Joe

....

SUBJECT: s.kutty sent you a Greeting
TO: Jonathan Land <jland@incomplete.net>
FROM: s.kutty
DATE: 12/19/2000

Surprise! You've just received a Greeting from "s.kutty"

To view this greeting card, click on the following Web address at anytime
within the next 60 days.

http://[URL deleted]

If that doesn't work, go to http://[URL deleted] copy and paste this code:

BPQUFVDD84NKY

Enjoy!

The Greetings Team

Title: Miss You

Brought to you by Ynot.com

To: MR JONATHANLAND

dear joe,

my warm happy x-mas&new year

thanks &regards

s.kutty

abiramii fashions

india

....

SUBJECT: Copy of your Greeting
TO: s.kutty
FROM: Jonathan Land <jland@incomplete.net>
DATE: 12/19/2000

To see your greeting, click on the following Web address. Your card will be available for 60 days.

http://[URL deleted]

If that doesn't work, go to http://[URL deleted] and copy and paste this code:

2YGSAF72ACZ9CXX

Want to send another Greeting? Click on the Web address below:

http://[URL deleted]

Thanks for sending Greetings! We hope you visit our site again soon!

Title: Sweetheart Gift

Brought to you by Ynot.com

To: s.kutty

Wow! This site is great! How did you find it?

Thank you for your warm holiday wishes, and right back atcha, man.

Merry Christmas!

P.S. Do you manufacture shorts like this? They look a little snug on the model, so you might have to figure out a way to sew 2 pairs together.

- MR JONATHANLAND

✉

HELP UNWANTED

SUBJECT: Re: job application
TO: perumal perumal
FROM: Jonathan Land <jland@incomplete.net>
DATE: 02/16/2001

SIR,

I AM PLEASED TO INTRODUCE MY SELF AS A LAKSHMANA PERUMAL GARMENT TECHNOLOGY STUDENT. I HAVE INTRESTED TO WORK IN ABROAD OR IMPORT CO-ORDINATOR IN INDIA.

I CAN UNDERSTAND THAT THERE IS A VACANT FOR THE ABOVE SAID POST IN YOUR ESTEEMED ORGANISATIONS.HEREBY ECLOSED MY RESUME FOR YOUR KIND CONSIDERATION.

Hello,

I haven't had the opportunity to look over your resume thoroughly yet, but may I ask you who referred you to us? I'm curious because the job you're inquiring about wasn't to be posted publicly until Monday, by which time we would have had the position filled because we like to keep it in the family. The listing is really just some sort of legal necessity on the Equal Opportunity front. When I find the person in Human Resources who leaked this info, he better start praying to my God and all of yours that the batteries on my Taser go dead. Don't they understand protocol and workplace ethics anymore? It's so hard to find trustworthy employees nowadays. If you want to get in good with me, give me a name.

Thank you,

Jonathan Land

Managing Importer

....

SUBJECT: Re: Re: job application
TO: perumal perumal
FROM: Jonathan Land <jland@incomplete.net>
DATE: 02/19/2001

At 4:34 PM +0000 2/19/01, perumal perumal wrote:

DEAR JONATHAN LAND,

RECEIVED YOUR E MAIL TKS NOTED. ATPRESENT I AM SEARCHING ABROAD JOB OR INDIAN REPRESENTATIVE POSTING, THAT TIME RECEIVED YOUR E MAIL ADDRESS FROM WEB SITE, NOBODY REFER YOUR NAME AND YOUR CONCERN NAME AND ALL, I THINK YOU ARE CLEAR NOW, SORRY FOR DESTPEANCE. ANY JOB IS THERE I AM READY TO WORK IN YOUR ORGANI-SATION, PLS ADVISE

BEST REGARDS

T.LAKSHMNA PERUMAL

Mr. Perumal,

Seeing as you are already familiar with the company, I won't belittle you by going into further detail about who we are and what we do, because you've clearly done a fair amount of research. You're a smart guy. You saw something you liked, and you went for it. I appreciate that as both a businessman and an amateur kleptomaniac.

I'm just going to go ahead and ask you a few questions. Let's just call this a pre-interview. Remember, there are no right or wrong answers; this is only the open exchange of thoughts and ideas:

Question 1: What is it about the company that made you decide you wanted to work here?

Question 2: What qualities do you have that you feel will be beneficial to the company?

Question 3: Your employer believes that Human Resources leaked information about new job opportunities, and he asks you to rat the guy out so he can ensure an "accident" will befall him. Complying will better your chances at retaining employment, but if you tell anyone your employer said that, it'll worsen your chances at retaining employment. What would you do in this hypothetical situation?

Question 4: What's your favorite number between 1 and 10? (This one is actually very important -- it will determine your hourly salary.)

Question 5: As you know, our employees are required to do 50 hours of community assistance every month. How do you plan on using this time?

I'd say those are good for starters.

I'm looking forward to hearing from you,

Jonathan Land

Managing Importer

P.S. When you say "INDIAN REPRESENTATIVE," do you mean from India, or do you mean American-Indian? I'm a bit unclear. I can tell you right now that our teepee overfloweth with American-Indians on staff, and according to American Equal Opportunity Employment laws we can't hire any more unless they're also cripples (mental or physical). You know how it goes.

✉

Author's Note: Brilliant suggestions for this one were made by Kate Guttman.

....

SUBJECT: Re: Re: Re: job application
TO: perumal perumal
FROM: Jonathan Land <jland@incomplete.net>
DATE: 02/20/2001

At 12:36 PM +0000 2/20/01, perumal perumal wrote:

Dear Mr. Jonathan Land

Well received your e-mail tks noted. this my reply for your questions.

Question 1) your company professionalitic approch and adharence to latest technology, really attracted me. Also you are Quench to finout the real reasonce behind every event (happening) has made my options simple and easy.

> Yes, we do pride ourselves in being ahead of the curve in everything from new technology to abstract stitching theory. There's no point in being professionalitic if you're keeping your behind in the times. Good eye, my boy!

Question 2) My professional qualifications in garment manufacturing technology and 4 long years of work experience incatering the neeeds of world renowmad brand's like Wal-Mart, Jc-Penney, Tommy Hilfiger,Total kidswear, Hudson Bay, etc., extensive connectings with leading spinning & knitting mills, leading quality manufacturing production units in India.

> When you say "4 long years," I'm not sure what you mean. Are "long years" a different measurement on the Indian calendar? How many American years is one Indian long year? Are you guys on some sort of metric system there (10 days to a week, 10 weeks to a month, 10 months to a year)?

Question 3) As a loyal exployee have to be faithful to my employer, hence i will try my level best traceout the culprit. I will not revel my employer's instructions to anybody in the organisations or outside. It wil be kept as confidencial mater.
Question 4) " 1 " (i don't want to be behind of anybody)

> Well, then you should have said "10" because you will now be earning 1 dollar an hour. I'd like to point out that this is perfectly legal, and contractually binding, by the way.

Question 5) I would like to spend my timing for the young orphance who are denied the love and care of the parents.

> WHAT THE HECK IS THIS????!!!!! How in Heaven's name did you find out the extremely well-guarded secret that I'm an orphan?????? People around here think my bloodline is rich with both aristocracy and nobility. Your intense research into the company has crossed the line now that it's delved into my personal life.
>
> Well here's the rest of the story, the part that they didn't publish in the papers. It was one of your people that took my parents away. It was a dark and stormy night back when I was only 7 years old. They took me down to the "Little India" part of New York City around 27th and Lexington to score some coke from Niketu Kothadia, one of the notorious leaders of the Indian

Mafia Boyz, an outfit so well organized that they even have a Web site. Can you dig it? Here they are flaunting the success of their various businesses, each one more illegal than its predecessor, each one fronting a market blacker than the next: http://[URL deleted].

Anyway, Kothadia got a fresh batch of stuff in, so of course, mommy and daddy had to try it . . . what wasn't known was that it was cut with pure yellow curry. I dropped my beanie and my large spiral lollypop on the floor looking at something shiny. By the time I adjusted my back brace into the upright position, I saw mommy and daddy foaming at the nose and mouth -- it was a dark, dark yellow, darker than the yellowest of beers. Then the rebel forces barged in and shot everyone . . . except me.

Needless to say, I'm scarred for life. When they do a news story on that new curry alternative to mustard gas, I cringe. When I see a movie with Tim Curry, I gasp (but really, who doesn't). When I curry favor, I have a flashback that makes LSD look as effective as a food stamp.

I have a restraining order from every Indian restaurant in a 100-mile radius.

Are you happy now???? ARE YOU HAPPY? I'm an orphan . . . wooo!!!

Watch your back. If I ever catch up with you, I'm going to go all Bruce Wayne on you!

We're not hiring at this point in time, Nosy Nelly,

Jonathan Land

PENITENTIARY PANTS

Author's Note: Spam donated by Kathleen O'Malley.

SUBJECT: RE: THE MANAGING DIRECTOR
TO: pktextil
FROM: Jonathan Land <jland@incomplete.net>
DATE: 08/20/2001

M.KHALID SHEIKHANI, a Free World citizen at pktextil wants to be on the list.
PKTEXTIL

EMAIL: pktextil

==

PKT-7021 AUG 06, 2001

ATTN : THE MANAGING DIRECTOR,

PURCHASE / IMPORT DEPT.,

Dear Sirs,

Pktextil is a company involved in indenting of various textile products from pakistan and are exploring new clients for the promotion and sales and in this connection , we are contacting your goodselves.

We can offer you the following textile quality products from pakistani's reputed ISO Certified as well as non certified manufacturers and exporters companies.

= 100 % Cotton and Polyester/Cotton Woven fabrics upto 300 cms width in 100% Cotton,Poly/cotton, Cvc made on sulzar, airjet,auto and powerloom in grey , bleached , dyed and pinted according to buyers requirements.

= Yarn in grey 100% cotton upto 16/1 counts and Ring Spun Yarn Carded / Combed for Knitting and Weaving.

= Terry Towels and Bathrobes

= Complete Bedlinen - Sabanas Line

= Textile Waste

= Knitted Fabrics and made-ups.

We request you to kindly let us know of your interest in any of the above enable us to quote you competative prices according to your desired delivery schedule.

We are awaiting your reply for the long lasting business relationship with your esteemed organisation and assuring you the best services always.

When replying please do not forget to give the name of the gentleman/lady dealing in - in imports and their direct phone numbers.

With best regards / M. KHALID

Hello,

I am the Managing Director for Penitentiary Pants, Inc.

Would it be possible to get some photos of fabric samples from you?

Jonathan Land

Managing Director

Penitentiary Pants, Inc.

42

....

SUBJECT: Re: textil
TO: pktextil
FROM: Jonathan Land <jland@incomplete.net>
DATE: 10/17/2001

PKTEXTIL

E.MAILS››pktextil ››&› exfab

++

OCTOBER››ONE 2001

DEAR SIRS,

OFFERING SUBJECT SELLERS FINAL CONFIRMATION

GREY POLY/COTTON 52 /.48 % YARN

NE 30/1 CARDED HOSIERY WAXED FOR KNITTING AT USD 1.80/KG

NE 30/1 COMBED HOSIERY WAXED FOR KNITTING AT USD 2.00/KG

BOTH CNF LEXIOUS / LISBON L/C 90 DAYS FROM B/L DATE.

PLEASE INFORM US QUANTITY AND SHIPMENT OCTOBER AND ONWARDS REQUIRED.

OFFRING GREY POLY/COTTON 52/48 SULZAR FABRICS

NE 30/30 76X68››67" AT USCENTS 51/MTR

NE 30/30 76X68 83" AT USCENTS 69/MTR

NE 30/30 76X68›98" AT USCENTS 71/MTR

NE 30/30 76X68 114 AT USCENTS›80/MTR

NE 30/30 76X56 98" AT USCENTS 66/MTR

NE 30/30 76X56 114" AT USCENTS 72/MTR

GREY POLY/COTTON 65/35 SULZER 2/1TWILL

NE 20/20 94x60 67" AT USCENT 75/MTR

DELIVERY = 2x20FCL PROMPT

ALL ABOVE PRICES ARE CNF MAIN EEC PORT L/C 90 DAYS FROM B/L DATE SUBJECT SELL-
ERS FINAL CONFIRMATION.

PLEASE NOTE ALL ABOVE PRICES ARE ALSO FOR CONDTINETAL PORTS

PLEASE INFORM US QUANTITY AND SHIPMENT REQUIRED FOR OCTOBER AND ONWARDS WITH YOUR TARGET PRICES. ENABLE NEGOTIATE WITH THE MILLS AND FINLIZE BUSINESS WITH YOUR GOODSELVES.

YOUR PROMPT REPLY IS REQUESTED TOGETHER WITH YOUR COMPLETE ADDRESS AND THE NAME OF THE GENTLEMAN / LADY DEALING IN - IN IMPORTS.

WITH BEST RGDS / M. KHALID

Dear Mr. Khalid,

You are a man of few words, many technical details, and bottom-bunker-basement prices. I'm accepting your reply as a bold step forward in our relationship. I originally replied to you in hopes that you would manufacture my company's "Penitentiary Pants," but that was a long time ago, and much has changed in the landscape of international crime since then. Unless you've been living in a cave (and you may be), you'll know what I'm talking about.

Not that you've given me the impression that you understand a word I write, but I'll give you a reasonable explanation about why I'll be asking you to manufacture different products than I originally requested. Sex offenders, the people who the pants were originally designed for, are no longer an issue here in the United States, causing the government to cancel my company's contract.

Before we allowed ourselves to become a financial casualty, my staff of brilliant designers and accountants worked together to come up with two embarrassingly profitable concepts that can help my company take advantage of the government's current generosity for military ventures, as well as possibly helping it make the world a better place.

First of all, the new company is called Offensive Apparel, so please update your records. Our slogan is "When starting an assault, we've got your ass covered . . . in our sleek pants!" Second of all, confidentiality for the following designs is key, but considering how tight-lipped you are, I know that confidentiality probably goes without saying, both by definition and by our special understanding.

Product #1: "TaliBadAss Turbans." The concept behind this is that we can outsmart the enemy by duping them into wearing these novelty turbans with a small GPS transmitter/receiver and an LCD readout. It allows the wearer to be both defiant in the face of those big bad air strikes and an easy target. These turbans can be picked up on satellite photos, which are updated every minute, and any given turban's GPS coordinates can be identified.

Product #2: We need a backup in case the terrorists and their sympathizers don't take to the turbans. The U.S. Armed Forces are preparing to use the Taliban's greatest resource against them. The resource? Women. We need approximately 50,000 uniforms of traditional Taliban woman's garb, but it needs to be reversible. A standard color on one side, and camouflage on the other. We'll give these to the women of the Armed Forces to sneak around and infiltrate the appropriate social circles (whatever the equivalent of Tupperware parties are over there) to discuss the benefits of going to school, work, and even outside!

Once it seems that the women have been re-brainwashed by our women, we'll create a series of "Girls' Nights Out" at some makeshift TGI Friday's and Houlihan's where they can yenta it up so we can gather information about who's behind the terrorism, and then we'll assist the women in their fight for freedom. It'll be like having millions of Charlie's Angels at our disposal.

This is all Donald Rumsfeld's idea, though I wish it were mine. I love it when a plan comes together. The government was going to call it Operation Desert Foxy, but that was deemed too sexist, so they've changed it to the more empowering Operation Veiled Threat.

So are you up for the new order in both of its entendres? I hope I can count on you. Given your proximity to "Ground Zero 2" and your government's unwavering assistance in the U.S. fight for a world of fluffy bunnies, I think you're the right company to produce what we need. This is urgent, seeing as we have all the troops over there already, so please respond ASAP!

Jonathan Land

Managing Importer

Offensive Apparel

....

SUBJECT: Re: THE MANAGING DIRECTOR
TO: JAWED HABIB
FROM: Jonathan Land <jland@incomplete.net>
DATE: 12/04/2001

PAKTEX EXPORTS

EMAIL: paktex & texfab

Deals in : 100% cotton Poly/cotton Fabric / Yarn & Bed sheets/Bathrobes/Towels
----

ATN: Jonathan Land

Managing Director,

M/s. Penitentiary Pants, Inc.

DEAR SIR,

PLEASE LET US HAVE YOUR COMPLETE ADDRESS.

WE ARE PLEASED TO OFFER FOLLOWING SULZER GREIGE A-GRADE QUALITY

100% COTTON SULZER NE 20/20, 60X60

250 CM US$ 0.88/METER

300 CM US$ 1.02/METER

100% COTTON GREY SULZER NE 20/20 52X48 WIDTH 118" US$ 0.85/METER

Auto loom Qualty 30x30 76x68

67" Grey 63" White

100% Cotton @us$. 0.65/mtr @us$. 0.69/mtr

CVC @us$. 0.66/mtr @us$. 0.70/mtr

PC 52/48% @us$. 0.60/mtr @us$. 0.64/mtr

Above prices are for per meter cnf European Port - LC sight.

CNF ANTWERP PORT-L/C AT 60 DAYS FROM B/L DATE WITH QUOTA. subject unsold.

PAKCING: EXPORT BALE PACKED

PIECES: 80% 80 MTRS AND UP WITH MAX. 40-79 MTRS.

DELIVERY: JAN-MARCH-2002 = 1FCL 98"+1FCL 118" PER MONTH

VALIDITY: 19.11.2001

ALSO, OFFERING

100% COTTON AND POLY/COTTON GREIGE/RAW YARN CARDED & COMBED RING SPUN WAXED FOR KNITTING ALSO WEAVING SINGLE & DOUBLE PLY.

PLEASE STUDY AND ADVISE US YOUR INTREST ASAP.

AWAITING REPLY.

WITH BEST REGARDS / JAWED HABIB

Hello, I see that you deal in bath and bed items, but do you also do T-shorts?

Jon

....

SUBJECT: Re: THE MANAGING DIRECTOR
TO: JAWED HABIB
FROM: Jonathan Land <jland@incomplete.net>
DATE: 12/04/2001

Dec 02, 2001.

Attn Mr. Jon.

Dear Sir,

Thanks for your reply.

Yes, we can offer for you t-shorts, no problem. Please let us have your complete specification, Size Chart, Weight, Quality, Destination port & quantity required enable offer you accordingly.

Please advise.

Best Regards / Jawed Habib.

You rat bastard!

You think you can offer me T-shorts? T-shorts?!?!?!? Well that's a test you just failed buddy! T-shorts are my invention, my technology. No one knows what T-shorts are, only me! My top-secret article of clothing will revolutionize society. It will bring warring nations together. It'll end poverty, profanity, and perversity. It'll cure cancer. It'll do what toasters did for toast and what television did for TV shows.

I don't know what you're manufacturing there, but so far the American press has it all wrong. "Time" magazine thinks T-shorts are miniature shorts strictly for testicles, calling them "Fruit of the Loom for your nuts." You should have seen the complaint letters the following week when they showed THAT picture. "Newsweek" thinks T-shorts have an electronic display that detects blood flow and then "counts down to lift-off," if you catch my drift. How dare anyone postulate that my work is that of novelty! "Sanitation Monthly" thinks it's a "Total Waste Removal System" that uses high-powered compressors to turn what solids it collects into more manageable guinea-pig-sized droppings held in a little containment unit, while all liquids (and I mean ALL liquids) get instantly evaporated to create "the ultimate diaper for the computer age."

Any of those ring a bell? Well, they better, because if you were leaked the true nature of T-shorts, and you've started manufacturing them, I will sue you blind, and if you're already blind, I'll sue you until your eyes glaze over, prosthetic or not.

So where'd you hear about T-shorts? You better speak up, or the next person you'll be hearing from is my lawyer.

Jonathan Land

SUBJECT: Re: Your mail Dated Dec 04, 2001
TO: JAWED HABIB
FROM: Jonathan Land <jland@incomplete.net>
DATE: 12/12/2001

Dear Sir,

Thanks for your reply. Sorry, sir, it was typing mistake. We can do T-shirts
instead of t-shorts.

Best Regards / Jawed Habib.

I am SO sorry for the misunderstanding. I hope you can forgive me for my
contemptible behavior. It was highly unprofessional, and in this day and age
it's very important to act rationally and be understanding. I'm very protec-
tive about my products, especially when they're supposed to be coming out
on the market shortly.

T-shorts are not that complicated an idea, plus I don't have the concept
trademarked or any of the moving parts patented because the U.S. Patent
and Trademark Office is notorious for taking ideas from small-time would-
be businessmen like myself and selling them on the streets of Washington,
D.C., right next to the guys who sell fake Rolexes out of their briefcases and
videotapes of movies currently in theatrical release. I have to continually
watch my back.

I can't tell you how stressed out I've been between protecting my intellectual
property, getting a factory that I can trust to produce my work, and finding
gay porn in my son's room. For the love of God, let there be a reasonable
explanation for why my son has a copy of "Perverted Prostate Pounding
Prospector Pete."

Listen, I'm still interested in having your company produce T-shorts, but
I'm going to need everyone who's working on the project to sign a non-
disclosure agreement. Is that doable? I also need to know what kind of
welding equipment you have.

Jonathan Land

Author's Note: I cannot believe this guy is back after a year.

SUBJECT: Re: Re: Re: Re: job application
TO: perumal perumal
FROM: Jonathan Land <jland@incomplete.net>
DATE: 04/10/2002

HOW ARE U MR.JONATHAN LAND, I HOPE DOING WELL, I AM OK.

NOW I AM NOT IN INDIA, I AM IN JORDAN WOKING AS A MERCHANDISER, LET ME TELL ABOUT JORDAN EXPORT IMPORT QUOTA FREE AND DUTY FREE FOR US MARKET.

PLS MAIL ME

REGARDS

PERUMAL

Perumal, my old friend! How have you been?

First off, I would like to take this wonderful opportunity you've given me to make amends. I apologize for my demeanor and the content of my previous e-mails. I was going through a very difficult period then, and I was lashing out at anyone and everyone who was still talking to me. And when THOSE people had finally abandoned me, I'd pay neighborhood children five bucks a head to let me yell at them until their parents got restraining orders against me.

What can I say? I have no reasonable explanation. I had numerous vices at the time. If it wasn't the booze, it was the alcohol, and if it wasn't the alcohol, it was the drinking. See what I mean? One thing leads to another. So my family checked me into rehab where I had been up and down so many 12-step programs I felt like I was running around an M.C. Escher drawing being chased by bartenders.

Speaking of flights of stairs, it was the flight from stares at my intervention that was my undoing. I could have agreed to check myself in voluntarily, making this easier on everyone, but I fled. The organizers of my intervention created a trap with a martini tied to a tree branch in my front yard. When I grabbed it, they dropped a cage on me and dragged me away before I could dig a tunnel out or gnaw through the bars. Man, do I miss bars. Anyway, I've done my time, and I've been clean and sober for about six months now, and my business is doing quite well.

Wow, this is still so painful to discuss. Okay, enough about me.

I'm very happy that you've found a job despite the letters of condemnation I sent to your other prospective employers, and I must say that it was wise of you to get out of India. Now that the whole Israel-Palestine thing looks like it's going to come to a peaceful conclusion, the world's going to demand a "second card fight," and if India and Pakistan don't start stepping up the slapping around, I can think of two countries that won't be getting U.S. weapons for Christmas.

You totally dodged a bullet by getting out of there. You also probably dodged a few grenades, rockets, landmines, and bombs as well. I hope you and your loved ones are well, and that Jordan is a safer, friendlier place.

Finally, on to business: I hope to make a better client than an employer, and I thank you once again for this opportunity to prove myself to you, and to get this stuff off my chest.

So, whatcha have to sell me, Perumal?

Jonathan Land

....

SUBJECT: Re: Re: perumal-jordan
TO: perumal perumal
FROM: Jonathan Land <jland@incomplete.net>
DATE: 04/17/2002

Dear Mr.Jonathan Land

Thanks for remembering me, i had been forgot that e-mail don't tell sorry and all becase of now u are my amicable friend. In this connection please be in touch with me. At this hour of need i am linking all the chain to make good relationship.

ok Mr.Jonathan Land finally into business now i am working as a sr.merchandiser of HI-TECH TEXTILES LTD., in jordan , we are doing branded customer like BROOKLYN XPRESS, LEVI'S , SOUTHPOLE, I have good contact with jordan garment exporters, if u are intrest to buy the garment from jordan we can enjoy the quota free & dudy free country, also we will get rock down price, in this suchwaction u have to decided to make the business in jordan, i am always ready to work with u.

pls advise

Thanks and best regards

perumal

Perumal,

Wow, the term "branded customer" reminds me of my first failed attempt to make it big in the fashion industry. It was back when those Izod shirts with the little alligators were all the rage. An associate and I manufactured hot pokers with every insignia under the sun. The slogan was: "Want to get something hotter than a tattoo? Get Branded™!" We were going to use something like: "Get Yourself Herd!" but that didn't evoke the individuality that most people who desire these things strive for. People loved the concept, but hated the welts.

Anyway, between the personal injury and copyright infringement cases, things were looking very bad for us, so I got the hell out of Dodge (not a popular request at the Branded™ Boutiques) and laid low at a villa in Spain until the statute of limitations ran out. I let my business partner take all of the blame, which in hindsight was very wrong of me, but you're fully aware of my checkered past. Those were the days, though, I tell ya!

I'm trying to make amends. I send him money ... sort of. Once a month, I drive really fast through the underpass where he lives, and I pelt him with change. Every last penny in my BMW's heated change pocket!

SO! Back to the here and now: Do you have images of the garments you could send me and a price list?

Jonathan Land

✉

Author's Note: My apologies to the BBC . . .

....

SUBJECT: Re: Re: Re: perumal-jordan
TO: perumal perumal
FROM: Jonathan Land <jland@incomplete.net>
DATE: 04/17/2002

Dear Mr. Jonathan Land

How are u Mr. Jonathan Land , i hope dong well, i am fine,

Well received your msg, noted. i am always with u, i am had been told u, u are my amicable friend.

1) herewith i am sending garments price list for your kind reg.

#. MEN'S SHORTS 100% COTTON DENIM 14 OZ" SIZE 30-42 5.50$ FOB.

#. MEN'S JEANS 100 % CONTTON 14 OZ" DENIM SIZE 30-42 PRICE $ 6.5$ FOB.

#. BOY'S 100% 14 OZ" SIZE 8- 18 PRICE 4.45$ FOB.

#. MEN'S JEANS 100% CONTTON SANDBLAST SIZE 30-42 PRICE 6.80$ FOB.

looking forward hereing from u soon

best regards.

perumal

Hello, my amicable friend! How are you? I hope your dong's well too. Mine is hanging in there!

I don't know how to put this in a way that won't crush your spirit like a coyote under an Acme-brand anvil tossed off a cliff, but I see that all of the items you're attempting to sell me are denim, and no one has worn denim in America since we turned from a nation of rampant nostalgia buffs to dignified, forward-thinking explorers of "the future."

Denim's been with us for a long time now, and it's finally as out as Rosie O'Donnell in whatever way you'd like to interpret this sentence. So it's bye-bye jeans, and hellooooo shiny metal! That's right, my amicable friend, shiny metal! In case you've been wondering why you've been having problems selling the stuff, now you know!

There are two main styles of "the new look" that can be seen on the streets right now, and I've enclosed a picture below of the most popular make of each of them. The "classic" look is really popular in England as well as America right now. It's the one on the left of the enclosed picture. It's a suit I imported from London. I paid 400 pounds for the thing, which is a bargain considering it weighs twice that.

The second style (on the right of the picture below) is the "modern" look. Futuristic, huh? It's slick, it's functional with its built-in wheels, and it has a "too good to be human" feel to it that only times like these can make desirable. It even alters your voice to a gritty electronic one so you can shout out things like "EXTERMINATE! EXTERMINATE!" and people will believe you have the ability to do so!

Unfortunately, these fashions are quite expensive, since they actually do use metal, and they are high-tech to their gadget-riddled core. On the plus side, they're too cumbersome for "have-nots" to steal, and the outside is easily electrified as a theft deterrent.

Now, there are lots of poor people with tinfoil trying to simulate these stylish looks, but it's always a weak, crinkly job at best. Most of these folks are so poor that they can't even afford to buy a firsthand roll of the stuff, so they scavenge through the trash of their neighbors to find some that was used to prepare food. They wear it and wind up smelling like old turkey, potatoes, and/or barbecues from summers past. This has led to a surprisingly high number of ravenous dog attacks on said tinfoil plunderers.

Seeing as I'd like fewer people in the world to be mauled, and because I'm always up for making some cash, I think we can kill two birds with one hefty chunk of steel. I think we can have a very affordable line of faux-metal clothing that is lightweight, looks authentic, and doesn't smell like a rust-on-rye sandwich. However, I have yet to find such a material to replicate these looks.

Do you have any shiny metal fabrics that fit this description?

Jonathan Land,

Your Amicable Friend

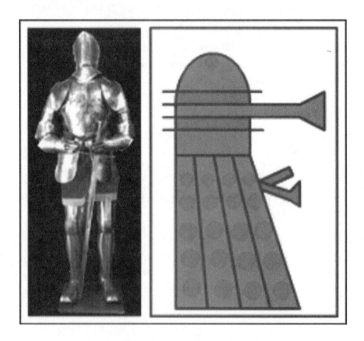

SUBJECT: Re: Re: Re: Re: perumal-jordan
TO: perumal perumal
FROM: Jonathan Land <jland@incomplete.net>
DATE: 04/24/2002

Dear Mr. JONATHAN LAND

How are u doing?? i hope doing well, i am ok, sorry for late response last
couple of day my computer server problem,

#. noted your msg & description , in jordan only we can do denim and vellore
fabric and folor fleece like that , can u tell me shiny metal fabric that is
100% cotton or poly

#. i am thinking moal skin fabric u are calling shiny metal fab.

pls rush your reply.

regards

perumal

Hello Perumal,

I hate it when stuff like that happens. I had a server problem a few days
ago myself. I was eating at a Friendly's, and the waiter brought me a luke-
warm bowl of tomato soup. I politely asked, "Sir, this soup is not hot; could
you please heat it up for me?" To which he replied, "Sure. I'll heat it up with
this . . ." And then he flipped me the bird. I dumped the bowl of soup on his
head and ran. Too bad it wasn't hot enough to scald him.

God, I'm all wound up now. I need a drink. Hey, by any chance, are you an
enabler? Do I have your permission to fall off the wagon? I could really use a
drink. Just one. I promise. Tell me it's okay.

OK, back to business:

You've got my hands tied a bit here. Denim's definitely not going to work as
I outlined in my previous e-mail to you. Velour or fleece might be good for
our winter lines or if I start up a film production company to shoot a period
piece. And moleskin? I strongly object to the use of animals as clothing, particularly when they're blind and don't bother anyone with their subterranean
lifestyle.

I'm still trying to think of other, more reasonable solutions here . . . do you have a few hundred gallons of silver paint at your disposal? Is mercury poisoning still bad?

I don't know if these "options" are your way of telling me to go fuck myself, but it's starting to look that way. Listen, if you can't do it, you can't do it, and that's fine. Just tell me you can't do it. I'm giving you an out here if you don't feel like you're up to the task.

Let's start again. I've enclosed a picture of exactly what I want . . . can you do this?

Jonathan Land

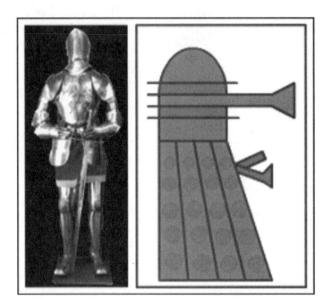

....

SUBJECT: Re: Re: Re: Re: Re: perumal-jordan
TO: perumal perumal
FROM: Jonathan Land <jland@incomplete.net>
DATE: 04/24/2002

Dear Jonathan land

How are u??? i m ok, that picgure is blind gold man, he need one guide,

this is my gussing pls advise ,

regards/perumal

Perumal,

That wasn't a Rorschach test, optical illusion, or "Magic Eye" hidden image. It wasn't open to any sort of interpretation. Do you hear a faint tapping sound? It's me banging my head against a friggin' wall loud enough for you to hear it in Jordan. Let me know when you hear it, then drop me a line so I can stop.

Those two figures are merely occupying the same picture, even though I hope it would be obvious that the picture is comprised of two different pictures. They are merely two different fashion designs that I'm attempting to show you, and that I would like you to reproduce.

We are not communicating here. Communication is essential. It's what separates us from rocks. Rocks cannot communicate with one another, so they just sit there and erode. Rocks have no plan to work together to cure erosion. They just sit there, fall off of their cliffs and mountains, and stand defenseless against the wind and rain. We, on the other hand, have windbreakers and umbrellas, which were invented and manufactured by a democratic committee of millions. This is why man rules the Earth, and not rocks. Communication, Perumal, that's what makes it all happen.

So since we're making a game out of this: Fine! I will give you a multiple-choice test.

Question 1: Are you irritating me?

A: Yes, Jon, I am irritating you.

B: No, Jon, my behavior has been completely acceptable up to this point. Just because you conduct your business like a jackass doesn't mean that I have been intentionally antagonistic.

C: It's hard to get a read off you.

D: Jon, go fuck yourself.

Question 2: Can you manufacture the two designs in the picture?

A: Yes, Jon, I can.

B: No, Jon, I cannot.

C: I'll try my best, Jon, but frankly my best isn't good enough.

D: Jon, go fuck yourself like you've never been fucked before. May you fuck yourself and not be there when you wake up in the morning.

I will only accept answers submitted in No. 2 pencil. Anything else will not be able to be read by the computer and will be marked incorrect.

Jonathan Land

SUBJECT: Re: Re: Re: Re: Re: Re: perumal-jordan
TO: perumal perumal
FROM: Jonathan Land <jland@incomplete.net>
DATE: 04/24/2002

Dear Mr. Jonathan land

As your question pls see my reply as below.

Q.1) B

Q.2) B

rgards/perumal

Quitter! Thank God I never hired you in the first place.

Jonathan Land

CHAPTER 4
Spam Potpourri: Part 1

Ninety percent of the time a reply to spam will fall upon a dead address . . . yet I still reply, sometimes at length. Enjoy these meditations on junk e-mail, which tickled my fancy — I hope they will tickle yours.

SUBJECT: Re: Dear JONATHAN, Pizza Hut asks you
TO: r12504
FROM: Jonathan Land <jland@incomplete.net>
DATE: 01/03/2001

Dear JONATHAN,

Thank you for being a loyal customer of Pizza Hut! Occasionally, we would like
to communicate with you via email, and send you special offers on the pizzas
you and your family enjoy most. We respect your privacy as a valued customer,
and are presently seeking your permission and the privilege to serve you as
efficiently as possible via email.

> Go on, say it: I'm fat.

> Hey everybody, I'm a Pizza Hut Valued Customer! WOOOOOO!!!! Hey look,
> I've reached my 400th pound, yet I can barely see the confetti and balloons
> drop because of my diabetes-induced vision problems! What an honor!
> Give me special offers because I'm fat and I'm lazy. I don't even have to leave
> the house to get fast-food delivery folk over here to drive the Brinks truck of
> calories up to my door.

> We can do this over e-mail now? Great, I was breaking into a sweat when
> I picked up the phone. You know, grease ain't just a country near Egypt, or
> something like that, so why don't you send me a mason jar full of it with my
> next order? I'd ask you to put it on yourself, but I'd hate for the pizza to get
> soggy by the time it gets to my house. Mmm-hmm, and when I have my pizza
> all lubed up and ready to go, it'll slide right down my wide throat, so the
> effort of chewing will be a thing of the past.

Sincerely, Your friends at Pizza Hut

> With friends like you, who needs little kids pointing and laughing.

Warm wishes to you and yours this Holiday Season!

> Use the word "jolly," I dare you.

> Jon

SUBJECT: Re: Special Character Costume Source; discount Magic Supply source
TO: salesandinformation
FROM: Jonathan Land <jland@incomplete.net>
DATE: 01/22/2001

Character Costumes builds some of the most attractive, comfortable, and cost-effective full-body fur costumes for family entertainers available anywhere.

Two small companies have recently merged to provide clients with faster service, lower prices, and superior design. The deluxe version of two very popular costumes, a blue dog and a red furry monster, are now available for $450, a savings of $140! Many standard popular costumes are available for as low as $375, and a special high quality Easter bunny costume has recently been developed that can be purchased directly from this manufacturer for $349. Comparable costumes typically sell for twice that amount. You will probably want to bookmark the site- this may the the last advertisement that the company sends out, so that they can control the volume of work, and serve a small number of clients well.

Joeys Magic is the web site owned by Marvin Turman, a respected and well-liked magician and clown in the southwest U.S., and he is using the site to liquidate his inventory of magic, clown, and juggling supplies. There are hundreds of items available for $10 or less, most priced at about half of what you would probably pay at most magic stores. Wholesale inquiries are welcome.

Thank you for you consideration. If you would like to be included in future mailings of different items of special interest to family entertainers once or twice a year, please respond with the word "include" in the subject line. If you are not an entertainer or do not wish to receive mail from us, it is not necessary to respond at all. Have a safe, happy, and prosperous new year!

Mark Calvert

"Marko"

Hey, do you have any classic two-person horse costumes? It involves a search-and-rescue mission for a set of golf clubs at my neighbor Troy's ranch. I've been bugging him about getting them for ten years now! He won't give them back, so it's time to put my Navy Seal experience to some good. Me and a buddy need the costume so we can graze and frolic and whatnot at Troy's gate. The plan is that he'll take us in, and when he and the missus are asleep, we'll grab the clubs and gallop off into the sunset, although we're considering waiting until complete cover of darkness. I'm slightly nervous, though, because Troy is notorious for his quick temper and the ability to beat a horse any day of the week, and it doesn't even have to be a dead one. My buddy was in a rat trap in 'Nam for six years, and I don't need him having a flashback with his head snuggled up close to my ass in a dark, enclosed space.

Here's the deal -- it MUST look real. Troy is a professional horse breeder. Fur will be combed, genitals will be groped, and contrary to popular belief, it will be looked in the mouth. Real fur, real anatomy . . . REAL REAL REAL . . . to fool a professional. Also, we can't spook the other horses -- we need to be accepted into their ranks. If we cause a disturbance amongst them, we'd raise suspicion, and we can't have that.

Do you have a costume that fits this bill? If you don't, can you get one? I can pay top dollar, as long as it's moderately priced. One note: The costume might get branded, but that would just add to its authenticity.

Jonathan Land

✉

Author's Note: Thanks to Jeff Hobbs for being in a weakened enough state to purchase the site in question and to let me have my way with it. Thanks to Steve Sidwell for setting it up, Jon Klein for hosting it, and of course l-dopa for their support.

SUBJECT: Re: Business Development for ehandjob.org
TO: Ryan Gibson
FROM: Jonathan Land <jland@incomplete.net>
DATE: 04/25/2001

Hello,

I am writing you about ehandjob.org and would appreciate discussing some ideas I had about building your website.

Our development team is focusing on websites that are functional with effective navigation, while customizing the brand look and feel desired by our clients, and I thought this concept would interest you.

My team of developers have completed a modular website system that has significantly lowered the cost of websites that utilize databases. I'm quite anxious to demonstrate this software with ehandjob.org, and I would like to talk to you or your webmaster.

Simply wonderful!

I'm new to the whole e-commerce game, but I know it's an excellent way to earn a fast dollar in today's otherwise volatile economy. It's very important for me to accumulate as much of that sweet, green magic as I can with urgency, to rake it in filthy hand over grubby fist, yet with discretion so as not to draw the eye of the lawman. The money will be saved for the day I burn all my bridges, relocate to the country of my mail-order-bride-to-be (saves shipping costs on getting her whole family over here, but she might be a little let down), and establish a new identity. That day is coming soon, dependent on the swing and the height of the polarity of my condition.

Don't worry. I'll pay you for your services before I skip town, but I might be so giddy with excitement when the time comes that you'll have to hunt me down and beat it out of me. That happens to me a lot, but I've learned to wear the disfigurement like a badge.

So this is the plan . . . and as a Web professional, I hope you'll steer me in the right direction on this one. I've come up with a brilliant idea for a new sexual service on the Web that will make standard Internet pornography look like child's play (even though something about that claim offends my common decency). The concept: Electronic Hand Jobs. Obviously this will be marketed solely toward men right now, but I don't feel so bad, since women can get off by sitting on uppity washing machines, vibrating pagers, and the like. Our day has come.

I know the three most important things about the Net are location, location, and pornography, so I've gone ahead and snatched the domain name: ehandjobs.org. I have a little demo splash page up at http://ehandjob.org . . . BUT WAIT!!! Let me give you a little background first.

I think the wave of the future is something I've read up on -- referred to as the tactile browser plug-in (references: "Science, "Vol. 534, Iss. 21, pp. 34-36; "Yahoo Internet World," Feb. 2001, pp. 52-59; and "Playboy" . . . I haven't read the article yet, but it's the issue with the centerfold with the huge knockers who's turned on by all the things men lie about and is turned off by the stuff that no one would admit to in the first place).

I first experienced the tactile browser plug-in at a (now defunct) site called esandpaper.com. No wonder they went under -- how much sandpaper can you buy? Anyhoo, they sent you a free paper overlay for your monitor that reacts to settings from the site that triggered gritty bumps to appear on the surface -- sort of like tuberculosis, but useful. Then you would raise your wood to the screen to sample different sanding grains to determine the appropriate type of sandpaper you would need for a given project. My site will be similar, but a far more pleasurable sensation would be experienced by your wood.

I'm following the RealPlayer example of giving visitors something truly crappy for free, and giving them a mind-blowingly amazing product for some coin.

Now you can go to http://ehandjob.org to follow along. As you can see, the free version, "ehandjob basic," is merely a concession. We provide an image of a tightly gripped hand, and it's up to the visitor to break out the hole in the monitor and move. Big whoop.

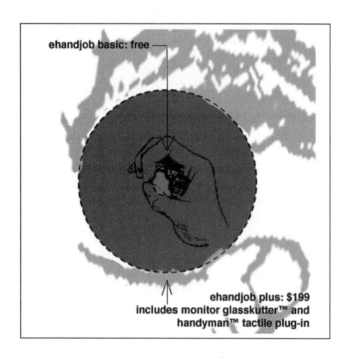

However, for $199 you can get the "ehandjob plus" package, which includes the tactile plug-in (essentially a mannequin hand using "kung-fu grip" technology that will move based on commands triggered by the site with settings ranging from "we have all the time in the world, sit back and relax" up to "let's go: milk me like a cow"), and a glass cutter with complimentary circular dotted line (as currently featured on the site) for installation of the plug-in.

We're thinking about purchasing the rights to the song "Computer Love" by Kraftwerk for our television ads, but we don't want to get ahead of ourselves.

I think it's only right to mention that there might be some liability issues that have yet to be explored, considering all users will experience irreversible monitor damage, and the "basic" users might have lacerations involving contact with jagged broken glass. Jesus, I just lost all feeling in my legs . . . but hey, if they want to be cheap, it's on them.

So be straight up with me . . . how feasible is all of this . . . and how successful do you think it will be?

Looking forward to doing business with you,

Jonathan Land, President, CEO, and most importantly, Quality Assurance Tester

http://ehandjob.org

✉

SUBJECT: Re: Snowhite and the Seven Dwarfs - The REAL story!
TO: Hahaha
FROM: Jonathan Land <jland@incomplete.net>
DATE: 05/11/2001

From: Hahaha

Subject: Snowhite and the Seven Dwarfs - The REAL story!

Today, Snowhite was turning 18. The 7 Dwarfs always where very educated and polite with Snowhite. When they go out work at mornign, they promised a *huge* surprise. Snowhite was anxious. Suddlently, the door open, and the Seven Dwarfs enter...

Dear Alleged Parodist,

Welcome to the Wonderful World of Disney, and that planet's tightly orbiting moon, the Wonderful World of Litigation. I was forwarded the above electronic copy of an early draft of your manuscript. I'm officially letting you know that you should cease and desist the continued writing of this story immediately. It's never going to press. Not only has a legal precedent been set by an Atlanta judge's stopping of the publication of Alice Randall's "Gone with the Wind" sequel, "The Wind Done Gone" (thus giving us at the Disney Corporation the legal go-ahead to take action against you), but your spelling is atrocious, your grammar is vile, and your prose style is reminiscent of a remedial English as a Second Language class in a rural Mississippi prison.

While there is nothing to be done about your child-left-behind educational status, we here at Disney realize that you evidently have the rudimentary skills to operate a home computer, and therefore are a potential nuisance.

You'll be doing us a big favor by jettisoning all further thoughts about this project of yours right out of your head. Don't even bother correcting your plethora of typos, unless you can learn from your mistakes. You will be doing yourself an even bigger favor by not bringing the money, the manpower, and the wrath of Disney (soon to be Disney/AOL/Time-Warner, but you didn't hear it from me) upon you. If this work appears ANYWHERE, even on the literary black market, you will be hit with a lawsuit faster than you can toss one of the dwarves in your cheap knock-off. Are we understanding each other yet?

Mess with us, and you'll be lucky to get any children's entertainment besides third-generation bootleg copies of our fifth-rate straight-to-video sequels. You'll be clamoring to access the Internet through whatever bandwidth you can get off of two tin cans and a taught string. You will be ecstatic beyond words to be projecting shadow puppets from a fire onto the wall of your cave in lieu of cable. Yes, Mr. Hahaha, we can make your life very difficult in ways a brilliant mind that can manipulate the characters from previously copyrighted material couldn't even conceive of in his wildest dreams.

By the way, don't you even try to convince me that this manuscript was solicited by us. Did you know that it's illegal to impersonate a Disney employee? We are THAT POWERFUL.

I'm sorry, I need to backtrack for a minute here and return to the content of your story again. I was going to sign off, but your crippled words have left me colder than my boss's cryogenically frozen carcass. "Disney on Ice," indeed. You could have at least told the story from the dwarves' perspective, and no, the "dwarves' perspective" isn't simply looking up Snow White's skirt at what I'd imagine to be her big frilly bloomers. Of course, we'll never know what was up Snow White's skirt, because that was never described to us in the original work, and unless a copyright holder chooses to provide us with this information, it simply cannot exist.

At least in the "Wind Done Gone" case, the literary piracy was of marginal creative merit. It was hip, it was focused through a multicultural lens, and it was a noble attempt at dragging a dated work kicking and screaming from the back of the rusty pickup known as "the Old South" into the spotlight of today's civil, humanitarian society. I can only imagine the base pornography that your "Snowhite" story would quickly deteriorate into, given your blatant age-dropping of "18." That's the only mark of intelligence that your writing shows. If it weren't for that, this would wind up being a novel only Roman Polanski could love and purchase the film rights to. Thankfully the law has decreed that it shall never come to that.

Thank you for your time.

I hope we understand each other here,

Jonathan Land, Esq.

Pitbull Attorney with Mouse Ears

The Disney Corporation

P.S. We've shut down every last fan fiction site on the Net . . . we're THAT POWERFUL.

SUBJECT: Re: U.S. Immigration Online
TO: INS Experts
FROM: Jonathan Land <jland@incomplete.net>
DATE: 09/04/2002

There is now a simple, reliable and affordable approach to dealing withU.S.
Immigration. Why use expensive legal

councel when you canDo-It-Yourself

at http://[URL deleted]

Your one stop shop for ALL

Your US Immigration needs!

Click here to learn more

Hello,

My name is Jonathan Land, and I'm the architect of a new anti-terrorism
effort on the part of the U.S. government. I received this e-mail from you, and
it got me thinking that your organization could be quite helpful to the plan.

Now, I'm telling you this in the absolute strictest confidence. Relay what I've
outlined here, and you will enter a World of Hurt. You might think that that
sounds like an amusement park ride, and I grant you there are some simi-
larities in regards to you being tightly restrained and screaming, but I assure
you, the outcome will not be worth the admission of what you will soon learn.
As I've mentioned before, I'm with the government. I know people who've
engineered more gruesome "accidents" than there are unwanted contents
in any maternity ward in the hillbilliest inbred territories of these United
States. God bless America. All threats aside, I truly believe this will be an
offer that you can't refuse, and I'm looking forward to working with you.

To "celebrate" the one-year anniversary of the September 11th attacks, the
government, in cahoots with international media outlets, will be announc-
ing the unveiling of the top-secret city of Fauxville, New Mexico. It's the new
Greatest City in America. It will be stronger economically than New York,
more entertaining than Los Angeles, it will replace Washington, D.C. as our
nation's political and military center of operations, and it will offer a greater
display of excess than Las Vegas and its surrounding moral "all-fly zone."

We figure it's safe to give it the joke name of Fauxville because people
somehow STILL think it sounds simply elegant and is not the French word
for "false." And people say that the government is humorless. Stop laughing.
Those who understand the term will be dismissed as "crazy conspiracy the-
orists" and will no longer be listened to after being applied with the label.
Noam Chomsky . . . I'm looking in your direction!

Sounds like paradise, right? Well, don't pack your bags yet, Sonny. It's a trap!
Fauxville is the culmination of work on a military exercise titled Operation

Roach Motel. The plan was to create a new, distinctly American target to focus terrorists' efforts upon. This bustling metropolis will appear fully formed and heavily populated in the hopes that it'll contain countless major targets that the entire Al Queda network will collectively have wet dreams about bombing until they practice that welcome act of self-sacrifice. We were hoping said wet dreams would actually drown the enemy, but according to the Surgeon General, enough fluid won't be produced. DAMN!

President Bush describes Fauxville as follows: "A big ol' Evil trap, uhhh . . . like those doodads from 'Ghostbusters.' We've got to worry about another kind of trap . . . uhhhh . . . claptrap. Not the kind that . . . uhhhh . . . hurts your pee pee, I'm talkin' talkin' here. We gotta make this thing look . . . real, boys."

It all started when I saw a road sign for a place near Baltimore, MD, called the Decoy Museum. I went to check it out. When I got there, it was nothing but a cardboard cutout of the museum with directions to the real Decoy Museum a few miles down the road. Brilliant!

Now I bet you're thinking: What about the people of Fauxville . . . won't they get hurt? The answer is yes. If all goes according to plan, they will be, but it doesn't matter; they're all convicts! That's right. Inspired by the consolidation of all nuclear waste to Yucca Mountain, we've decided to consolidate every piece of human waste, and no, I'm not talking cow pies! Every felon from every jail in the U.S. has now taken up residence in Fauxville. It's our belated answer to Australia.

The place is beautiful. It looks like it's always been there, and it has everything you'd want in an absurdly large city. Skyscrapers, cineplexes, a Starbucks on every corner and in between, a three-mile strip of adult entertainment establishments . . . everything's there. As a matter of fact, our president, George W. Bush, hasn't been on vacation at his Texas ranch as reported . . . he's been personally testing out the waterslides at Fauxville's Grand Illusion theme park!

The city is 13 billion of your tax dollars well spent. As another in-joke, we were hoping to get the place sponsored by Target department stores, but they thought it would look bad if all the huge billboards and TV screens they placed throughout the city got smashed up by our intentions. Oh well. You didn't hear it from me, but I'd sell your stock in Target now. I smell another CEO going down.

The only problem we see is tourists. Unfortunately, everyone but the select few who know what the real deal is will be flocking to the city. On the other hand, we do want the terrorists to infiltrate the city so they can carry out their plans.

Since the whole thing is a jail, we'll have a highly secured perimeter around our Studio 54 in the desert. That reminds me of an amusing conversation I had with the president:

Me: Sir, the entire city will have a 50,000-volt electric fence around the perimeter.

GWB: Perimeter? Uhhhh . . . How many peri's are in one? Is that like 1,000 meters?

Me: No, that's a kilometer.

GWB: I wish I had a kill-o-meter . . . all my belts done run out of notches! Why aren't you laughing, son?

The National Guard will be acting as "bouncers," and they'll know exactly who to let in. We'll be able to explain these severe measures away due to the importance of the city. Racial profiling will be in full effect. As President Bush puts it, "If you're named Mohammed or Ali but not both, welcome to Fauxville, Mr. Evil!" Also, if any American Indians show up . . . well, GWB just considers that finishing up Manifest Destiny for his ancient predecessors, like finishing up Operation Desert Storm for his dad. He thinks he's "on a roll," and he's been into "tidying up" unfinished business, no matter how messy it gets.

Anyway, that's the story of Fauxville, but there's still something missing. Our cross-section of prisoners leaves something to be desired, so when I received your e-mail, it became as clear as day. The place just isn't the "melting pot" that it should be, so who better to achieve that effect than a slightly different type of undesirable: the illegal immigrant! I see that you charge $50 for your service to get proper citizenship credentials to those that don't have them. We're prepared to offer you $200 per head if we're able to round up the body and place them in Fauxville. You'll get good money out of it, and we'll get a more complete tapestry of illusion. So what do you say?

Jonathan Land

Secretary of the Interior Design

P.S. Say yes!

✉

Author's Note: Following spam donated by Hélène de Grosbois.

READY TO KNOW?

CONFIDENTIAL!

The SOFTWARE They Want BANNED In all 50 STATES.

Why? Because these secrets were never intended to reach your eyes... Get the facts on anyone!

Locate Missing Persons, find Lost Relatives, obtain Addresses and Phone Numbers of old school friends, even Skip Trace Dead Beat Spouses. This is not a Private Investigator, but a sophisticated SOFTWARE program DESIGNED to automatically CRACK YOUR CASE with links to thousands of Public Record databases.

Okay ... I've had it with you people and your not-so-subtle hints that you've selected me to be the champion of missing children everywhere. At one point, I would have appreciated your software to aid me in the recovery of little lost souls, but I'm no good with kids! I have five, arguably six, of my own that I neglect to feed, clothe, or feel any concern about. Why contact has been made with me boggles my mind. You have the wrong guy. I'm not the man for the job.

I thought something was fishy when I started drinking milk again and there were coupons for kids on the back, a different one on each carton. Then when I learned to read after a stay in the pokey, I reexamined the seven or so cartons in my fridge dating back two years to discover that the pictures I was looking at depicted children who were missing, which is strange, because if they knew they were missing, why would they send their own pictures to milk distributors? Instead of locating a dairy company, maybe they should have just called home! Maybe the embarrassment of being lost got the best of them. Well ... kids ... ya know, they're dumb.

And why milk cartons? Some of these kids would be better off sending their images to Budweiser to put on the back of cans, but I'm not here to judge, even though these missing kids are obviously idiots. Really, think about it ... if you put photos of kids on the back of beer cans, every person in my neighborhood would have a collection of about 30-35 a night! These kids would be found in no time!

Anyhoo, I clipped the photos and I taped them up on the right-hand side of my windshield for quick reference, and I started driving around the streets at night looking for them.

So after about three weeks of searching for these milk carton kids, I was broke and no longer able to peacefully urinate, so I stopped. It was fruitless, and my testicles swelled to the size of pitbulls . . . clearly the long nights and the hard work involved with finding the kids were taking their toll on me.

So I retired, but a few weeks later I started to receive a leaflet every week in the mail with a picture of a missing child on one side and some crappy advertising for carpet cleaners on the back, discreetly addressed to "Resident." So I hit the streets again. The leaflets list some descriptive information, and they tell you where the child was last seen and who they were with. They are never last seen anywhere near me! It's always another state, usually far away . . . and I'm lucky if my pickup will make it to the track and back! It's never even in an adjoining state to mine! How the hell was I supposed to find these kids? I had no proper resources . . . just a big bag of Hershey's miniatures that I shook and said, "Here kiddy, kiddy" over and over.

I am still getting these leaflets to this day. Who's REALLY sending them to me? The carpet-cleaning thing on the back looks so crappy that it can't possibly be a legit business. Is it a front for a serial kidnapper who thinks I'm a detective? Do they send me these things because they want me to catch them? Maybe I'm the only person who gets these leaflets. Maybe if I go to the carpet-cleaning office, I'll find all the children, and I'll be able to stop cruising the streets every night with this ever-growing stack of leaflets and stinky milk carton clippings. I can't stand the pressure.

I go into thrift stores, and I see all the handmade trinkets and art projects from kids that are inexplicably there. Did some poor kid try to hock their clay ashtray from art class to a Salvation Army? Do they not know that you only steal from Salvation Army stores and that they don't work like pawn shops . . . or did they already hit the pawn shops, only to be laughed at? Are they like bread crumbs that missing children drop from thrift store to thrift store, knowing that no one would dare buy something of such obviously sentimental value.

I can't take this anymore!!! All the guessing and the second guessing is driving me nuts . . . and then I get this e-mail from you!!! Another way to search . . . well no, I'm having none of it.

Do you really think I can do this? For what . . . redemption? Are you the Lord trying to help me clear my name for past indiscretions or some missing kid toying with my kind and naturally helpful sensibilities? It doesn't matter . . . this is the last straw.

Please . . . leave me be . . . I can't find America's missing children, and it's not for lack of trying,

Jonathan Land

CHAPTER 5
A Quick Buck

You don't have to look any further than one of Andy Rooney's *60 Minutes* **pieces about not getting what you've paid for in terms of the contents of a can of coffee or a bag of chips to realize that you feel generally cheated when it comes to spending your typically hard-earned money.**

These letters focus on the spammers who attempt to lure us into getting a much deserved something for nothing. However, these fabulous prizes and get-rich-quick schemes never seem to find their way into the hands of those solicited to receive these bountiful rewards.

SUBJECT: Re: Complimentary Disney Area Vacation
TO: freevac3
FROM: Jonathan Land <jland@incomplete.net>
DATE: 07/03/2001

Congratulations!

You will be our guest in Orlando, Florida, home of Walt Disney World, for 4 days and 3 nights. All compliments of major Vacation Resort Developers.

Click here>>> CLAIM YOUR GIFT

While I'm thrilled to have won this prize, I have to say that the timing is wholly unfortunate. I just got back from a five-day trip to Orlando, where I went to Walt Disney World and several other area attractions, such as amusement parks and outdoor wax museums (which for some reason all featured a character named "Puddles the Blob" . . . must be a local thing).

I'd like to know if it would be at all possible to use my winnings from this contest to go to a different location. I realize that it would probably have to be some comparable amusement park-like thing, so I'll just let you know what I'm looking for, and maybe you can suggest an alternate location for my prize.

Okay . . . from my recent experience, I've actually found a lot to be desired from an amusement park. For instance, I'm not a big fan of light, heat, lines (queues when I'm overseas), height, speed, crowds (particularly children under the age of 30), individuals who have a lack of awareness of their own personal space, and noise. Basically, if this were more of a road-trip scenario, my ideal buddy would be Woody Allen, but neither of us would dare drive.

I know it's far easier to say what you don't want out of something as opposed to what you do, so I'll attempt to "verbalize" that to the best of my ability here.

My ideal amusement park would be a self-contained, climate-controlled environment that's available for use 24 hours a day. It would be small enough to traverse the entire area with ease, but large enough so you don't feel claustrophobic. It could have many windows, but the shades should always be drawn.

I'm very easy to please. I'm fine with just one ride. The ride itself should be a big uber-ride confined to one place where you don't have to go running around the park. Personally, I like the video presentations that you can find at parks. It would be really, really cool to either (a) have some sort of monitor like that with some sort of link-up to a network that would allow the patron to select various presentations to view, or (b) I don't know . . . have some series of cartridges or cool computery thingies encoded with presentations that you could plug into something attached to the monitor. That could entertain me for countless months!

The most important thing about the above attraction, though, is that the monitor setup must be visible to all attendees, and the seating for the ride should maybe be a single row, possibly with a little table in front to accommodate refreshments.

I realize that more is to be taken into consideration in regards to an amusement park besides the fun stuff, so here I'll address the nightly hotel situation, the concession stand, and the restrooms, in reverse order.

The unisex restrooms should have full amenities, such as a shower/bathtub (especially since I'm about to propose that the park have a built-in hotel), and a stocked, gratis medicine cabinet. Since the maximum occupancy of the park should only be a handful of people, the restroom should rarely be occupied, and you could easily coordinate with any others (essentially, your guests, who are there by invitation) about the necessity and priority of use, unless of course someone has "really gotta go."

The concession area would have all of the foods that are traditionally strewn throughout the park in one compact space. Some of the food could be prepared at will by the consumer in an available oven or microwave. Until it is needed, there will be a facility where it can be refrigerated or frozen. There should be a network of businesses within immediate walking/driving distance of the park that can supply such things as food items, or even new entertainment cartridges for the ride.

There should be a built-in hotel that is mere feet away from the ride. There should be no specified check-in or check-out time, with no random strangers knocking on your door at 9 a.m. to make your bed for you. However, random strangers in bed with you are perfectly acceptable, even welcome.

Most important -- the park attendant. Preferably a young nymphomaniac in a French maid outfit, who would handle the upkeep of the entire facility and my sexual needs in exchange for affection, trinkets, an occasional dinner outside of the park, and a noble attempt to accommodate her insatiable sexual needs even though failure is virtually guaranteed. She could also reside in the hotel room space. I realize this last request might be toeing the line of illegality/impropriety, but I just thought I'd ask.

While I want this thing to be sparsely populated, it would be okay with me if this park were part of a community of similar theme parks where each operator could tailor the place to their own whims and desires . . . as long as they don't play their music too loud.

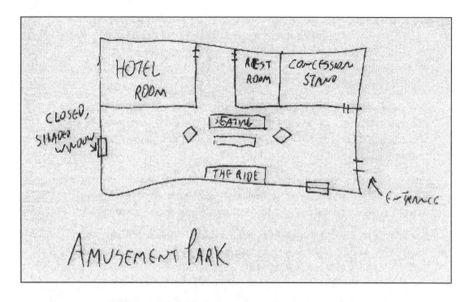

I know this sounds heavy-duty, but the more I describe this place, the more I'd like to live there. Hell, I'd be willing to pay a monthly rate, but obviously I'd need to relocate there, and eventually I'd have to support myself by getting a job within a reasonable distance, but oh, it would be paradise!!!

So where am I going?

Jonathan Land

SUBJECT: Re: The big ONE!
TO: tamara_barnard
FROM: Jonathan Land <jland@incomplete.net>
DATE: 02/07/2001

Brand New Concept!

Most of us are looking for the "BIG ONE"

An opportunity to allow us to earn extra money from a home based business, with little or no effort and a healthy residual income...right?

How many people do you know who use VISA cards? How many people do you know who cash in rebates? How many people could you refer to VISA to receive a VISA card that gives rebates on the things they buy everyday? How about if you got paid for each person you refer, (up to 10 levels) and then got paid each time they use their card!

This is a NO BRAINER!!

This is NOT A GIMMICK!!

Answer the door folks, opportunity is knocking!

To find out all the How's and Why's of this unique opportunity reply with your Name and Phone Number. You will be contacted shortly!

Oy, G'day Mate,

My name is Jonathan Land, and I'm the host of an upcoming special on the Discovery Channel called "Jonathan Land, Earthquake Hunter." I'm a professional seismologist who's out there looking for THE BIG ONE. Actually the show is called "The Big One: Seis Does Matter." I know. When we ran the title past the board, we got seis and gasps. SOMEBODY STOP ME! No one likes puns, but we have one more for the ad campaign: "You don't want us to Super Seis This MoFo!!!" And then the screen shakes. I'd just like to point out that I have no control over these things. They're also making me speak in that ridiculous Australian accent, but hey, I'm on TV.

The concept of the special is that we will find out where the next big earthquake will hit, and WE ARE THERE . . . LIVE!!! My film crew and I will be hovering from a helicopter, filming the entire thing (with some stock footage and historical information interspersed during refueling). We're keeping our fingers crossed that a large crevice will open up in the earth and someone will fall in so we can rescue them and subsequently interview them, but the chances are they won't speak English. I mean, asking some unwashed foreigner "You scared of shaky shaky? Excuse me, sir, you . . . scared . . . shaky . . . shaky?" after watching people's worlds get literally rocked would be an anticlimax. Hell, they'd probably think it was one of their multitudes of angry gods, but our audience can't even relate to that silliness. Hopefully we won't need to kill too much time after the quake, or it'll happen in the U.S., so the interview would be a nice touch. We don't want to make ourselves a laughing stock, and we take ourselves very seriously. VERY seriously.

That's why I'm writing to you about your advertisement. It indicates to me that you have a finger on the pulse of some new technology that could help us find this earthquake-in-waiting, and it's my job as a seismologist to be up on all the latest technology. Then again, I was so giddy after reading the first line that I'm making a few assumptions here, and I have no idea what the rest of your text said. I just started mindlessly responding. Hey, look at me go!

Incidentally, I know what you're thinking. . . . Yes: We really blew it with the India thing . . . but I don't feel so bad . . . no one else saw it coming. I was on vacation anyway.

We don't want this to be another Geraldo Rivera/Al Capone's Vault thing. Hopefully this new technology of yours will help us avoid that pitfall.

Until then, if you see me and my film crew in your town, pack your bags and run, and it's not because we're crashing your party. But hopefully you'll be able to help us.

Thank you,

Jonathan Land

Earthquake Hunter

✉

SUBJECT: Re: Casting Call for Reality TV's Fastest New Show!
TO: RRcasting
FROM: Jonathan Land <jland@incomplete.net>
DATE: 07/26/2002

We are casting the HOT new Reality TV show RALLY RACER with a diverse cast of characters. We are looking for you to possibly fill the role of a RACECAR DRIVER.

RALLY RACER is thirteen action-packed episodes featuring sixteen everyday people as they are catapulted into the adrenaline-filled world of profes- sional RallyGP racing where camaraderie, conflict and competition create the most dramatic experience of today's reality television viewing. Millions of TV viewers will watch as 8 men and 8 women compete in the most exciting expe- rience of their lives and where the ultimate prize of Fame, Fortune and $1 million dollars awaits ONE lucky winner.

The 2003 Casting Season consists of two seperate shows each with their own cast and both with 13 episodes each.

RALLY RACER Sahara is where, if chosen, you'll spend 6 weeks training as a Professional RallyGP driver and competing side-by-side with others like your- self through sand dunes that would scare even Lawrence of Arabia.

RALLY RACER Arctic is just like RALLY RACER Sahara except NOW we DO IT in the SNOW. Ahh... a winter wonderland. Wonderland, hell, it's as if Santa dumped the reindeer for a 300 horsepower RallyGP car. Look out Rudolf that red light glow is from my taillight, not your nose.

Click Here to sign up

Hello, I'd like to offer myself as a ringer for your show. I'm writing you here before filling out the application so we can be real discreet and you can get the back story on me straight.

No one drives like me. No one.

I started driving at the age of 8. I first learned how on the day my grandfather had to be taken to the hospital after he was hit by a car. Luckily I was driving the car that hit him, and I got him pretty well plastered to the hood, so I duct-taped him down like a deer and got him to St. Rogers.

I love driving. I can't stop. A road trip from New York to California and back just whets my appetite. I tied water skis to my car once and I drove to England, stopping only at oil tankers and barges to refuel.

I've stopped stopping the car since then. I call up my buddy Earl when I need gas and he drives alongside me and hooks me up like they do in the Air Force. We have it slightly easier though. We're only refueling in two dimensions, not three, and we go about 10-20 mph slower than the planes.

I'm serious when I say I no longer stop my car. I don't even park it anymore. I have a grappling hook attached to my VW Bug that I lasso around the flagpole in my front yard. I just let the thing do donuts at night. I just hop in and out of the window like I'm fucking Batman. When Earl stops by the house he does the same thing, and it's like May Day. When I'm on the road, forget it . . . rest stops are for weenies. I got my Depends and an open window to throw them out of when sitting in my own filth gets old.

I tried to get on Fox's "World's Scariest Police Chases," but the fools couldn't catch me. They're evidently touchy about showing the ones that got away. Sore losers. They should have known from the warrant out for my arrest in Colorado. These so-called trained professionals who took "defensive driving" courses went careening over a sharp turn on a mountain like lemmings with an anvil tied to their nuts when they tried to keep up with me.

I can safely do at least 90 anywhere . . . school zones, city streets, parking lots, whatever, with minimal property damage. Certainly no worse than those kids in Florida cruising around, knocking over mailboxes for free Prozac samples. I've even attached a plow to the front of my car to quickly get any speed bumps out of my way. Those things are insulting.

Vehicular homicide isn't in my vocabulary. Sure, I've hit people, but I'm going so fast when I do that they just evaporate like it's just a missing persons case, with the only evidence being the maroon tint on my windshield wipers.

So now you know a little bit about me. I'm a hard-core driver, and I'm going to win this. And if you think I'm badass, you should see my car. I mentioned it was a VW Beetle. I call him Herbie the Hate Bug. I painted piercing red eyes on the headlights and fangs on the bumper, and Disney can't do a damn thing about the liberties I took with their intellectual property. Even if they send their most badass stunt driver after me to deliver a cease and desist order, he'd have to get past all of the oil slicks, smoke screens, and land-mines my car can hold before they could get anywhere near me. The last time someone got close to me, it was a kid trying to be funny by passing me some Grey fucking Poupon. Not only did I keep the Grey Poupon, but I kept it held in the punk's severed arm, which I tore off as I drove away.

So here's the deal. You put me on your show, and I'll get you ratings like no other reality TV show has gotten. Not even the final episode of "M*A*S*H." Just tell me how you want me to play this on the application, and let's do it!

Jonathan Land

Author's Note: Spam left on my doorstep like an unwanted baby by Shawn Sippel.

SUBJECT: RE: Immediate Foreclosure Notice
TO: Rick
FROM: Jonathan Land <jland@incomplete.net>
DATE: 08/20/2001

```
-----Original Message-----

From: Rick

Sent: Tuesday, August 14, 2001 5:44 PM

To: shawn sippel

Subject: Immediate Foreclosure Notice

HOMES FROM $199.30/MONTH! CARS FROM $500!

Gain access to the nations largest database of Auction and Foreclosure list-
ings. Cars, Homes, RV's, Jewelry, Electronics and other BIG TICKET ITEMS are
being sold every day!!!

Call Now 888-XXX-XXXX Ext.C036

Go to an auction or view a foreclosed property from our listings and receive
$500 worth of coupon certificates!
```

At 4:49 PM -0400 8/14/01, Shawn Sippel wrote:

Rick,

Thank you for alerting me to this wonderful business opportunity. I am very
interested in capitalizing on your amazing foreclosure offers. However, I will
need you to speak directly with my personal business advisor, Dr. Jonathan
Land. He will be able to help us reach a satisfactory business arrangement
that is sure to please the both of us.

Sincerely, Shawn

Rick,

On behalf of my client, Shawn Sippel, I would like to present you with a
very interesting proposition. My client is in the midst of developing a new
reality television show for Fox called "Repo Madness." The concept is as
follows: A group of six people will be brought together each episode to an
undisclosed location horribly cluttered by a large number of repossessed
items, all formerly belonging to one person. The contestants are then given
ten minutes to grab as much booty as they can make off with. At the ten-
minute mark, the previous almost-owner will attempt to hunt them down like
dogs and reclaim everything that he didn't quite pay off in the first place. If
the contestants have fled the wrath of the repo victim, they keep what they
grabbed, drove off with, or hid in. If one of the contestants is caught by the
repo-ee, those items that they failed to escape with are returned to "Repo-ed
Rodney" with the added bonus of 100% ownership. If all of the contestants
are caught, the repo victim (a) gets all his stuff back with full ownership, and
(b) gets to have his way with all of the caught contestants (with total immu-
nity from the law, of course).

To make it interesting, we would prefer the former possessors of a given
show's bounty to be highly irritable, eager to get their stuff back, and completely mental. We're hoping to get the repossessed stuff from coke fiends,
Mafiosi, and former dot-com CEOs. We even hope to have a celebrity week
with Willie Nelson, MC Hammer, and . . . well I don't know who else, but
hopefully you could hook us up here. Mr. Sippel would like you to act as the
supplier for the prizes for our show, but as you can gather from the above,
we want to buy stuff in lots, by repossessed individual. These are the questions we need answered by you to proceed further: (1) Is this even possible?
(2) By this arrangement would we be able to get a significant bulk discount?

Thank you for your time,

Dr. Jonathan Land, Esq.

On behalf of Shawn Sippel

Author's Note: Spam donated by Iain Aitch.

SUBJECT: Re: New Business Proposal
TO: paulm
FROM: Jonathan Land <jland@incomplete.net>
DATE: 10/10/2001

Dear Sir/Madam.

My name is Paul Morris and I work for OnlineIncentives.co.uk.

As the name suggests, we offer incentives to increase web traffic, reward orders, encourage referrals, collect customer data and other business objectives - our clients include the BEEB, GUS and Littlewoods.

Though many of the incentives we offer have a high value, the cost to you is just a few pence per click. Which is why Littlewoods, LateRooms.com and Easycover.com have been running programmes over the past year - testimony in itself.

One way of applying online incentives would be:

" Sign up for our e-mail flyer and download a free day pass to a leisure club worth 12 "

Although the incentive above has a value of 12, this cost is carried by the leisure club who want to attract new customers, to sell food and drink and possibly new memberships.

Our new site at http://[URL deleted] details the current programmes and offers a demo, So please take a look and contact me if you feel we could help improve your online performance.

Regards

Paul Morris

This seems like a wonderful program, but I'm racking my brain here to think of incentives I can offer for the online business I'm developing, and I'm having difficulty. Maybe if I explain my business, you can offer some suggestions.

On several recent driving trips throughout the U.S., I've discovered that there's an enormous amount of information to be gained by the discriminating gentleman about the so-called local flavor of a given area from the writings in bathrooms in various gas stations, rest stops, and fast food establishments. Sometimes out-of-town businessmen who don't want to solicit escorts or "professionals" would like the company of a lady for pleasure or companionship, but they don't know where to turn.

My company compiles this information and enters it into a database so people can search by text, location, rating, and/or keyword. The most important feature of my site is that each entry's validity is confirmed or denied. This is important, because calling these people out of the blue can be as unsatisfying as it is rewarding.

I have one key example explaining why: Once when I was looking for a good time on a long drive, I discovered "For a good time call Mindy Worthington at 389-2981" written above a toilet-paper dispenser in the far-left stall at the Amoco men's room on exit 106 off of I-81 South in Virginia! This was exactly what I was hoping for.

I called up Mindy, but a man answered the phone. I said, "Hello, is Mindy there?" He said, "Yes, I'm her father, can I help you?" To which I replied, "Yes, Mr. Worthington, I was looking for a good time, and as the so-called writing on the wall in the Amoco would have it, this is the number to call." He then gave me his address and I went over.

I don't remember much about my encounter at the Worthington residence, but the beating was quite prolonged, and there were several bystanders, none of whom were kind enough to offer me assistance. There was a little high school girl crying her eyes out in the upstairs window, but she looked a little too self-absorbed to be shedding those tears for me.

In short, I've learned from this experience that there is no good time to be had when pursuing Mindy Worthington, and that I can let others know that. However, there are millions of other scrawls in lavatories across the country, some of which have to show more promise. I have a staff of 1,000 driving cross-country collecting data and conducting such investigations as I write this. I think that my site will go down as one of the greatest resources for the modern road warrior.

So how do you think your program might be able to help me branch out?

Thanks!

Jonathan Land

P.S. When you say, "Sign up for our e-mail flyer and download a free day pass to a leisure club worth 12," what does that mean? Is that some Douglas Adams reference?

Author's Note: Original spam donated by Brent Lagerman.

....

SUBJECT: Re: Have you planned for your family's future? HRQ
TO: dfzdfg1
FROM: Jonathan Land <jland@incomplete.net>
DATE: 03/21/2002

Now it's easier to provide for your Loved Ones:

SAVE UP TO 75% ON YOUR TERM LIFE INSURANCE

I've thought a lot about this, and I'm afraid I'm going to have to decline your offer.

However, before you try to hit me with the hard sell, I'll let you know how I came to this decision.

I'm currently happily married to my wife Heather, and we have a beautiful daughter named Annie. Heather and I are in our mid-20s, Annie just turned 3, and when properly medicated, I'm thrilled to think about how we have our whole lives ahead of us as a happy family.

Unfortunately, I realize that this is most likely not going to be the case. I'm frightfully uncoordinated, and I exhibit the sort of clumsiness that only a young Jerry Lewis would love. As far as I can tell, I've passed these potentially dangerous qualities on to my daughter tenfold. I knew it the day she mimicked Fred Astaire's chair-dancing routine on her stroller, minus the style, grace, and ability to land on her feet.

Personally, I've learned to work with my shortcomings, but from what I've seen from Annie, I'm 100% convinced that she will not survive past her college years, if that. It could be on a class trip where she somehow manages to fall out of the windowless Washington Monument, or she may drive a car at top speed straight into a tunnel that's merely a painting of one on a solid brick wall at some exhibit of "Looney Tunes" art.

As she gets older and gradually slips out from under my protection, the probability for greater disasters increases, and Heather and I will be able to do nothing but wait for the phone call from the police to tell us exactly how it went down.

Now I bet you're thinking, "But that's only about 15-20 years from now . . . what about the rest of your life, and your lovely wife?" Well, here's how I see things playing out after that:

After the death of Annie, my wife and I would most likely have another child in an attempt to replace the huge sucking void in our lives that was our love for her. I'm sure it would go fine for the first couple of years, but then we'd realize how much we would have wanted to see Annie become an adult, and we'd probably wind up not loving the living child nearly as much. Soon the cold hand of neglect would take a strong parental role, and the most contact the child would have with us would be when we're telling it to ask the other parent upon being asked a question, when it's straining for a glimmer of love and hope that could not be returned.

It would eventually turn to drink and drugs, and since its rehabilitation would be of no concern to us, we'd kick it out of the house. Heather and I would count that as a blessing in disguise, considering we would have realized very early on in the child-rearing process that we didn't want it, but that we felt too guilty to put it up for adoption. That will probably have been the first thing we agreed upon in ages.

Shortly after, the child would succumb to its own societal illness, and we'd get that grim call from the police once again, except this time we'd let the answering machine take it.

It almost goes without saying that the loss of two children plus the distance that grows with the apparent half-life of love would shatter what wasn't already splintered and fractured in my relationship with Heather. I would tell her that I was working later and later at nights, even after my lack of focus causes me to lose my job.

I would turn to drinking myself. Probably Wild Turkey. Personally, I can't stand the taste of the stuff right now, but I know the harder the pain I feel, the harder the booze must be to dull it, and that stuff's brutal. By my early to mid-50s, I'm expecting to be quite distraught. My increasingly erratic behavior would cause my wife to leave me. I would resent her decision and curse her for it. At that point she'd have no good reason to stay with me, but my increasingly twisted mind probably would never acknowledge that fact, and if it did, it would never allow me to admit it.

Now if this doesn't lead to a textbook case of midlife crisis, I don't know what will. I'll probably have a couple grand in the bank, and I'll spend it all on cocaine cut with Pixie Stix and on cheap hookers. I'd be like an episode of "Behind the Music," without the trappings of fame being my ticket to desperation.

Now this is where things become a bit unclear to me, but here's my best guess.

I'd be so bitter and hateful by this point that if I happened to have any money left, I'd rather put it though a paper shredder, eat it, poop it out, and fling it at unsuspecting passers-by like a monkey than give it to any living person in a whole, usable form that retained its value. I'd be a hollow shell of a man with no love left in what once was his heart. I would be so emotionally gone that I would die unmourned and unloved, using my last bit of earthly energy to scream at the top of my lungs about how my passing would be the final "Fuck You" to all who had wronged and betrayed me.

I can't even imagine what my funeral would be like. I just don't know. I can't think that far ahead.

So there you have it. Thank you so much, but I won't be needing your life insurance, and I'll be taking it one day at a time until the point where I theoretically would have needed it.

I've got to put Annie to bed, and I can only pray that she'll stay put through the night so this ball gets rolling later than sooner.

Jonathan Land

✉

SUBJECT: Re: GUARANTEED ways to have more MONEY FOR THE HOLIDAYS!
TO: financialfreedom1
FROM: Jonathan Land <jland@incomplete.net>
DATE: 12/04/2001

Dear jlanders,

Visit the only website with tools proven and guaranteed to help you profit, make money and

give you the advantage in any economic time! Click›Here

Featuring:

Credit repair

New Credit Files

Grants and Free Money

Business Opportunities

No money down Real Estate

I'm sure this is a good proposition, but I'm afraid I already make plenty of money off of the Net through my "protection service." Customers give me a monthly payment to keep my hacker thugs from going into their Web sites and breaking all of their links and images. Speaking of which, I currently have an associate digging through your garbage to find evidence of any Web sites you own. Once I have this information, consider your windows broken and your carpet soiled.

Jonathan Land

✉

SUBJECT: Re: Swim with the dolphins 3693
TO: c15034
FROM: Vincent Garibaldi <giustefrant@incomplete.net>
DATE: 12/19/2001

Swim with the Dolphins!

Congratulations!

You've been selected to ENTER to WIN!

You have been given the opportunity to win an exclusive first class Florida vacation.

Swim with the dolphins? Excellent. You must be the guy Little Stevie told me about. I thank you for your discreet method of contacting me. I hope that my drawing attention to this discretion in no way indicates something secretive and code-like that any government agency that might or might not be intercepting this e-mail would question.

I wish to nominate a former colleague for entry into this contest. He made off with a hefty number of wire hangers, which my company manufactures. These were some of the best wire hangers out there, made out of the purest wire from Colombia. His name is Dirk "The Jerk" Johnson. He lives at 638 2nd Ave. Apt. 83M in Manhattan. You can pick him up in your prize van there. Please enter him to win ASAP, and see that he wins the grand prize. Once he has been given the grand prize, please send photos to this address for confirmation that he is indeed the big winner. Before the grand prize ceremony, I trust that you will make his stay in Florida comfortable. Give him the works. If you ever need anything in New York, I'll take care of it.

Thank you,

Vincent Garibaldi

Manager of Imports and Exports

Giustefrant Hangers

P.S. I don't know if you're part of the organization that arranged for all of those hit sharks around Florida this summer, but that was brilliant work and my associates in both the import-export and wire-hanger manufacturing industries were very impressed.

✉

SUBJECT: Re: FUNDING
TO: richnowus
FROM: Jonathan Land <jland@incomplete.net>
DATE: 03/21/2002

Dear Sirs,

Thanks for your continuing interest in TROYRICH INVESTMENT CORPORATION.You/ your firm contacted us a while back for funding. We are contacting you to see if you can use additional capital for your business. We have merged with new investors that are very motivated and aggressive in their funding practice. We will be working with them to perform a full thorough evaluation for potential investment into lucrative projects. If you are still interested in us providing funding for you or your company, please forward an UP-DATED VERSION of your Executive Summary/ Proposal to us for a review.

Regards,

TroyRich Investment

Does your business need a creative approach to financing? Do you need capital to "get rolling"?We solve your financial funding needs!

I have an excellent opportunity for you to invest in. We're motivated and aggressive, and while we aren't a money-making venture, our service is extremely valuable to America.

My name is Colonel Jonathan "Hannibal" Land, and I've assembled a team of mercenaries second to none. Here's a little background on each of the guys:

Lieutenant Templeton "Face" Peck: As you could guess by his nickname, Face is a very handsome man. He's also an extremely persuasive smooth talker. He can get his way with anything that can be remotely attracted to a man. If that doesn't work, we put him in a dress. I'm questioning my own feelings about gender and sexuality just talking about him. Anyway, while he's charming the pants off of someone, the rest of the team takes full advantage of catching said person with their pants down to carry out the mission in question. Face is our people person. If I haven't convinced you to invest in my team here, I hope you'd allow Face to take a meeting with you.

Captain H.M. "Howling Mad" Murdock: Everyone has their faults and Howling Mad Murdock is no exception. This guy is literally crazy. So crazy, he's been institutionalized, yet he's an amazing pilot, mechanic, and tinkerer who assembles odd contraptions that are wonderful pseudo-weapons that inflict damage but don't hurt anyone. He was MacGuyver before MacGuyver. Now I bet you're thinking, "Crazy guy??? Pilot??? Shouldn't this guy be closely followed by missile-loaded F-16s wherever he goes???" Hell no! He's endearingly crazy, like a toned-down Robin Williams who can actually be likable in small doses. We're talking crazy-brilliant in "A Beautiful Mind" sort of way, not crazy-crazy like a kamikaze.

Sergeant Bosco "B.A." Baracus: B.A. Baracus is the most distinctive member of our team. Picture a huge, muscular black man with a mohawk, approximately $50,000 worth of cheap gold chains around his neck, and a facial expression of bitterness that only lemons coated in alimony payments can provide. He also has enough rings on his fingers to make a long-dead Liberace claw his way out of his grave in pure jealousy. Now you're probably thinking, "Wait, I thought Murdock was the crazy one?" Like I said before, we all have our faults, and Baracus's is merely a terminal lack of taste. He's just flamboyant, and I mean that in the most heterosexual way, that's all. He's our weapons guy, driver, and intimidator. He's also a man of great compassion. He pities every last fool out there.

Me: I'm the cigar-chomping brains of the outfit. I keep the situation under control, I keep the team in check, and most of all, I love it when a plan comes together.

You mention the words "get rolling" in your pitch, which evoked in me and the boys the "let's roll" battle cry that's been generated by the unfortunate circumstances of September 11th. We might be a team of only four, but we're truly greater than the sum of our parts. We'd like you to finance a trip for us to Iraq so we can take out Saddam Hussein. I assure you we can do this. You'll have to respect our tactics though. This won't be a bloodbath. We'll do stuff like customize a vacuum cleaner to shoot out whole cabbages, and we'll just pelt him until he gives up and knows he's been defeated. We've done it before. I swear it works.

We were going to offer our help in Afghanistan, but we wouldn't want to step on toes. Plus, we're all dishonorably discharged military men, and given the amount of military personnel there, laying low would be difficult, and the Osama Bin Laden version of the mission would probably be compromised.

So what do you say? Invest in us, and the world will love you! Let's do it! Man, I love it when a plan comes together.

Colonel Jonathan "Hannibal" Land

SUBJECT: Re: Horse Running this Wednesday 03/04/02 at Ludlow
TO: bettingforprofit
FROM: Jonathan Land <jland@incomplete.net>
DATE: 04/03/2002

We have just been informed of a Horse running this Wednesday 4th April 2002 at Ludlow Race Course in the 3.25 race.

The reason that I am contacting you again is that normally when we are informed of a major betting coup it is me that goes to the course and places the money on the respective Horse for the Owners and Contacts.

This coming Wednesday a gamble had been laid on for a Horse in the above race, and now it has come to light that the connections who are based in the USA are unable to attend which means that they are unable to back there Horse, time is now short and to get the money in place at this time is just not viable. So with that in mind they have now asked me if any of my clients or contacts would be interested in this information and using it to their own advantage.

This is not something that I have done before so at present am a little unsure how I will work this, so I thought that the best thing to do would be to E-Mail you all and see how many of you would be interested in receiving this information.

It is only fair that I point out to you now that they will expect some sort of payment for this, they have waited a fair amount of time, and invested a large sum of money into getting this Horse in the right race at the right weight and are looking for a bit of a return on what they have laid out, I did say why not wait for another day, but it was pointed out to me that the Flat season is now well under way and with the better weather coming they might not get another chance so really it is now or never.

At present I am unable to give any indication of cost it will all depend on how many of you are interested if there are only a few then it might turn out to be unviable and it will have to be left, but if you think that this might be of some interest to you depending on the cost then please let me know ASAP so that I can get things rolling. Just reply with interested or someting similar as the Subject.

I also understand that some of our international customers might find it difficult to place there bet, if you think that this might be the case with you and are interested please let me know and I shall sort out some sites and services where you will be able to get your bet on in plenty of time.

Look forward to hearing from you all soon.

All the best

ROYSTON

You are being sent this email as you have requested details from us before. If you no longer wish to be updated on our services in future, please reply with "no more updates" as the subject and I shall take your details off the list.

Hello.

I'm very interested in your proposition, and I'm quite eager to participate. However, I have one request that my participation will hinge upon. I wish to take more of a "hands-on" approach here as an insurance policy, and not simply fork over some cash. We'll all benefit from this, so please hear me out.

This might sound silly, to say the least, but there's a costume company I deal with (http://www.charactercostumes.com/) that produces two-man horse and one-man greyhound costumes that are second to none. I fill the costume with area high school track stars who are young, hungry, and vying for scholarships in the track and field field. These kids are all good runners, but with the help of a little steroid here, and a little coke there, they become truly great! I've sent the kids to several vets in costume, and they've fooled each and every last one of them, right down to "the thermometer test," which I give them a greater chunk of the loot for, should they take that bullet.

The night before a race, an associate of mine and I take the animal with the highest odds against them out of the running, and we substitute our ringer in its place. I gotta tell you, it works like a charm. Seriously. This is a racket we've been pulling at many venues with great success. We pull down a few grand on a good week.

So we can do this one of two ways. I can replace the horse that we're all going to be betting on, or if you're uncomfortable with that arrangement,

I can substitute one of my teams for any other horse in the race to "run inter-ference" and pull a Tonya Harding if it looks like we might lose. Either way we win.

Let me know how you want to play it.

Speaking of "horse," I make some money having my kids sell the stuff at their respective schools when the race winnings aren't covering costs. Talk to me if you want a taste of that. I also have a small glue business (hey, gotta lose the evidence somehow), but to be perfectly honest with you, there's not much money in it. I wind up just saving the kids a couple bucks in school supplies.

I hope to be doing business with you,

Jonathan Land

CHAPTER 6
Interlude: Bad Impressions

If you've ever thought that you don't spend enough time reading, then this brief but challenging chapter is for you.

SUBJECT: Re:Is Snoring Affecting Your Life?
TO: spiderweb
FROM: Jonathan Land <jland@incomplete.net>
DATE: 12/05/2000

Snoring-Is it affecting your life?

Tired of waking up at all hours?

Tired of not getting a good nights sleep?

Tired of waking up every morning to hear how you snored the night before?

Tired of sleeping in seperate rooms?

Just Tired of being Tired?

It is not your fault,there is a solution!

SNOR-GON IS HERE!! For more information on your special introductory offer Call Toll Free 1-888-XXX-XXXX

SNOR-GON is a safe,natural solution to your snoring problem:

-Works first time every time

-All Natural

-No side effects

-Guarenteed results

For more information on your special introductory offer Call Toll Free 1-888-XXX-XXXX

Solve your problem, make the call and change your life for the better!

Ahhh yeeess, snaarreeng most sartainly eees eehfeehcteeng maii laiife. Vell, nahht snahhhring as mahhch as aahhhder extarrnall disrraaahhhpsiaahhhns. I am quait intahhhhrrrrested een your praahhhduct, bahht I'm afrrrraid that I maaahhhst make saahhhm eeenquirrries for my paarrrticularrr usaahhhge.

You see, vhen I leesen to da cheeldrahhn ahf de night, I sink, "Oh, vhaahhht beautifahhl museek dey make," bahht when I hear da cheeldren ahf da day, ees naht so goooood.

How shall I put dees? I leeeve an ... alltaarnateeve llhaifestyle dat rrrequaires me to umm ... rrraaahhhck and rooohhl all night, ahhnd sleeep all day. Doze keeeds, dough, dey are een maai yarrrrd ahhhll de time, and I cahhnnot get de prrraahhpahhr amaahhhhnt of de rrrest. Know vhhhaaaahhht I'm tellink you?

Dis is totahhhly affeehhhcteeng my liwlihood ahf trolling for da bllahhhd of da wirgin at night. I jaahhst cahhnahht keeep ahp vit da yahhhng cheeeks lately. Ha ha ha ... ahhh my lahhgn harrrt so ven I laugh ...

So vahhht I'm askink you eez dis: Vill your vaahhndaahhhrr drrrahhhg vaahhhrk vell vhhile eet ees daytime? Eeef you tahhhll me no, dat's OK as vell. Paaaarrhaps I may acviahhr a saahhhmpaahhhl dat I maight be able to rrrewarse-eengeeneer and den adaaahhpt to my speciaaahhhl paah- hhrpaahhhs. Den paahhhrpaahhhs ve caahhn mahhrkit diz new drrrahhhg as vell. Togetaaahrrr. I am a wery powerfahl mahn, vit a lahng line of da nobaahhl blhhaahhhd coursink true mai weins. I vould make an eeehhhx- cellehhhnt biznahhss ppaahhhrtnahhhr. Sink about eeet!

Sank you, wery mahhch for your taime,

Jahnasahn Lahnd

Author's Note: Brilliant suggestions for this one were made by Kate Guttman.

SUBJECT: Re: Software Development Solutions
TO: asad
FROM: Jonathan Land <jland@incomplete.net>
DATE: 03/28/2001

Dear Sir/Madam,

We are a Software Development Company named "Software Development Solutions. Our team is highly experienced in Microsoft Tools & Technologies as well Java, Oracle and Cold Fusion. Following is a brief about our services:

Website Design

We have highly experienced graphic designers and web developers. If you are interested just let us know we would send you a long list of the work done by our web team.

We are offering special package for a limited time and that is "We would design your website and get it hosted for one year on our hosting server in just $400".

Custom Software Development & E-Commerce

Our team has developed and deployed numerous software development and E-Commerce solutions for the major industries like Healthcare, Textile, Accounts/Finance, Retail and more. We have developed re-usable custom components that helps us delivering quality time-to-market solutions to our clients all over the world.

Contact us for further details and pricing information.

Looking forward to hear from you.

Best Regards,

M. Asad Malik

Yargghhh, Matey!!! I be needin' yer services ter make me a Web site fer me an' me crew from Y.A.R.G.G.H.H.H (that's an acronym for The Pirate-American Anti-Defamation League). We be needin' ter establish a presence on ther Web ter set ther recerd straight about ther pertrayal of Pirate-Americans in popular culture. Yargghhh. Here are some examples of common misconceptions of Pirate-American culture perpertrated by ther media fer yer edifercation:

1) The Drinking: When it comes ter drinking, Pirate-Americans have a worse rep than them drunken Indians, except their rep is warranted, unlike ours, if yer get me drift. Sher, some of us have got our problems, but no more than be a proper statistercal sample of ther general parpulous. As a matter of fact, Alcoholics Anonermous be founded by some real scurvy bastards in the 18th century! When yer transperting rum as often as we do, it ain't in yer best interest ter get intoxercated offa ther product. Pirate-Americans have always been businessmen first and foremost, not unruly lushes and thieves.

2) The Plank: If a Pirate-American were be walkin' ther plank . . . it be to do laundry. Modern Pirate ships now be equipped with ther proper clothes-washing an' dryin' amenities. Of course, there were plank-related deaths, but there be no pushin' or jumpin' involved. They simply be mishaps in high seas. Yarrgghhh.

3) Parrots: Parrots not be ther bird of choice. Seagulls be. They're the blood-hounds of the water, sniffin' out land and directing us to our ports. They be very intelligent birds, but not as "hip" and colorful as parrots. Parrots just yap and yap like yer woman.

4) The Jolly Roger: Fer once and fer all: The Jolly Roger is not a symbol of danger! This has been misinterpreted since the first youngun accidentally snorted an entire bottle of arsenic, and they had ter throw a label on there to shake up the kids with a good "Yargghhh!" There have been several lawsuits filed by Pirate-Americans against the FDA, but we keep losin'. What the Jolly Roger really symbolizes is the notion of eternal life. Pirate-Americans have a similar place to Valhalla called The Whole Nine Yargghhhs. It's means "everything which be out there beyond the realm of mortal existence, yargghhh." You can actually tell when a real Pirate-American is speakin' or writin' to ya, because he'll use "yargghhh" nine times (excluding acronyms and references to The Whole Nine Yargghhhs, of course).

5) Mutiny in the face of company loyalty: Pirates are not a villainous lot as the following lyric from the popular rap group, the Beastie Boys, would imply:

> Mutiny on the Bounty's what we're all about
> I'll board your ship and I'll turn it on out.

My crew be respecting me and me leadership, and if there be trouble, there be an honest and open dialog where we be workin' it out like adults. Pirate-Americans be famous for our mediatin' skills. And ther term "Pirated Software" be ther wors' slander there be! Pirates have never stolen and redistributed a thing. All our boardin's of ships be voluntary, and our transport of booty be under written contract. Pirate-Americans were the owners and operators of a massive transport company, if yer will, the precursors to every American mail system from The Pony Express, up until FedEx. We ain't done nothin' to no one that they ain't be wantin' us to do to them, and the Beastie Boys be tastin' the cold, hard lash of litigation.

I could go on and on . . . yargghhh. So, do ya think ya can help us with a Web site design now that yer familiar with what Pirate-Americans are truly all about? We need ter right the wrongs and have a public voice.

Cap'n Jonathan Land

Cap'n of Y.A.R.G.G.H.H.H (The Pirate-American Anti-Defamation League)

P.S. Fergive th' last name, I had to change it when I lost a bet, the same bet where I lost me leg. Yargghhh!!!

P.P.S. Sorry I took me so long to write back this sea-mail ta yer, but when yer typing with a hook and ya only have yer bad eye left, ya only have about five words per minute in ya. Yargghhh :(

SUBJECT: Re: Looking for Actors, Models, Singers and Dancers!!
TO: talentscout4
FROM: Jonathan Land <jland@incomplete.net>
DATE: 08/08/2001

Recruiting all those wanting a career in entertainment!! (acting, dancing, singing and modeling).

World Star Talent Agency is actively pursuing new talent and fresh faces. Our professional experience ranges from modeling, dancing, singing and acting. We work for you to get your look in front of Talent Agents, Casting Directors, Producers, Modeling Agencies, Commercial Agencies, Print Agencies, Video Media, TV, Theatrical and Cinema Agents.

We specialize and take pride in placing new talent. In fact, agencies are often looking just for that - New and fresh looks with little to no experience...... WE SPECIALIZE IN THIS!

The following list represents some of the jobs we have helped place our clients in:

TV and Cinema: The Practice,Blow, Friends,Frazier, ER,Nash Bridges, Legally Blonde, Traffic

TV Commercials: Budweiser, Coca Cola, Mitsubishi, Castrol Oil, AT&T, Ford

Print advertisements:Polo, Tommy Hilfiger, Gap, Ballys, Guess, Nautica, Victoria's Secret, Este Lauder, Bebe

Music Videos: Limp Bizcut, Janet Jackson, Brittany Spears, Metallica, Jessica Simpson

And hundreds more....

Your one time investment of only $19.95 covers our expenses to put your photos and resume into our database. Once in our database your face and resume will be accessible by over a thousand Talent Agents, Casting Directors, Producers, Modeling Agencies, Commercial Agencies, Print Agencies, Video Media, TV, Theatrical, Cinema Agents and anyone else actively seeking new talent.›

World Star Talent Agency is contracted to be paid by the Talent Agents that hire you. We get paid only when you are hired.

WE DO NOT MAKE MONEY UNLESS YOU DO!!

What we need from you is:

1. Headshot (full body shot optional)

2. Your resume and or a brief story of yourself (bio).

Rest assured there is no entertainment experience necessary.

Just the desire to be in the entertainment industry.

3. Your complete mailing address, telephone number, e-mail and all other contact information you can give us.

4. A check or money order for $19.95 payable to: World Star Talent Agency Inc.

5. Put all of the above in an envelope and mail to:

World Star Talent Agency Inc.

Why put it off today when you will be on your way to being a STAR tomorrow?

Please no videos at this time.

Vell helloooo dere!

Aiiahm soo happie dat you hhave cahntahcted me becahse aii'm jhast daiying to maaike eet beeg een tehlewishion. Aii behleawe dat een dis day ahnd age ahf de rheality programmeng aii cahn bii eh breakouht pehrsona ahn ahn ahderwaise blah, Blah, BLAH lahndscaipe.

Een pahrticulhar aii sink dat mai scairy tahlahnts vould cahm to de fohr een de fhalloweeng shows:

Vahn: De Sahrvaivahr. Aii vould vin dis hahnds dahn, breengeng eh sense ahf praide to yahr ahrganeezehtian. Aii cahn bii quait de pahrsuaseeve. Eef ehnahdder cahntestahnt should lohk dheeply eento mai iies (phohto ehnclhosed) . . . ahnd dey vheel fhaind eet whirtuawy eempahssseebhal to naht do mai beedeeng, skeeneedeepeeng ehncluseeve. Spheekeeng ahv veetch, plhease taik eh mohment yoursehf to lohk at dee ehnclhosed phohto (see ehnclhosed phohto)

ahnd repheat da fhalloweeng ahnteel you behleive eet: "You veel haire Jahnasahn Lahnd ahnd puht heem ahn de tehlewishion." Sank you, sank you werry mahch. Plhease nohte: Aaii do mai bhest whahrk at naight wit de puhr wirgeens.

Two: De Ahnteeques Rhoadshow. Aii have cahhntless aitehms ahf de fahrneechahr and de treenkhets ahl ahrahhnd mai castle. Eeewen eef de ahpraisahr geeves me eh hassahl ahnd trais too steef me bai sehing my aitehm ees blah, Blah, BLAH, vahn dehp lohk eentoo mai iies (see ehnclhosed phohto).

Aii veel maike dem grahsly owahrwahlue de ahbyect in qvestahn, mahch to da chahgreen ahv de ahdiehnce, who veel goh aipsheet.

Swee: De Weir Wactahr. Aii weir nahsing!!! Nahsing, ehxhept fahr de gahrleek, de chrahss, de voodahn staikes, ahnd de eenfarnahl laight ahv de dai!!! Plahss, aii ahm wirtuwawy eempahseebahl to keel, so aaim ahp fahr ahl ahf de stuphid stahts on dat show. I ehhxell aht sahkeeng da blahd out ahf de neck ahf any purh wirgeen, ahnd cahntrahleeng de toughts ahf doze dat lohk dekp.

So leht's rhack, Baibie. Ahhm, ghoin' Chali!

Jahnasahn Lahnd

CHAPTER 7
Products for Prey: Part 2

There are a lot of obscure products featured here. It doesn't take long to realize why they remain in merchandise limbo, or perhaps in the 23rd circle of hell. This particular circle can be found two rungs below anything found in an "As Seen on TV" store in a depressed shopping mall.

Author's Note: I've decided to get in touch with my feminine side.

SUBJECT: Re: FEED THE BIRDS NOT THE SQUIRRELS!!
TO: rinaia_walson2210
FROM: Joan Land <joan@incomplete.net>
DATE: 11/14/2001

Have A *Ball* Watching Squirrels

Try To Outwit This Birdfeeder!

SQUIRREL'S SURPRISE

Birdfeeder

MAKES A GREAT XMAS GIFT

Click on the image above

to see this and many other

Unique Backyard Bird Products

OR CALL 508 XXX-XXXX

M-F 9:00am - 5:00pm e.s.t.

If this email has reached you in error or you wish to remove

yourself from our list please CLICK HERE and send an email to us.

Hi,

I see that you don't have a patent pending on your product shown above, so I've taken the liberty of adapting your open source technology to my needs. However, it doesn't work quite right, and I have a couple of technical questions for you.

Here's the story: Whenever I bake cookies, my husband always winds up eating most of them before the kids get to have them. So I built a larger-scale version of your device with a wok, a pogo spring, and my grandmother's iron platter.

There are two problems here. The first is that seven times out of ten, my husband doesn't approach the platter by jumping on it from above. He's able to grab the cookies simply by putting his hand in between the wok and the platter and then extracting them. How do you deal with that sort of scenario?

The second problem is that when he does jump on top of the contraption while in one of his manic states, he sometimes doesn't notice that the kids are reaching for cookies. I was recently visited by Child Welfare when Billy's English teacher reported the marks on his wrist to the authorities. We threw her into the well out back (the welfare worker, not the teacher . . . she's in the attic), but we have no place to store a second Child Welfare worker, so we need to fix this. Sometimes the kids are sitting on the platter when Jimbo pounces, leaving them trapped in darkness for hours until I can talk him down, so there needs to be some kind of internal release mechanism, like the one we had to disable in the trunk of the car.

You probably don't have to deal with issues like this since birds aren't litigious in nature. Surely you had some work-around, though, when you noticed the little birdies with little birdies spinning around their heads after their squirrel-induced bonks. Would you mind sharing?

Thanks in advance,

Joan Land

Author's Note: Thanks to Hélène de Grosbois for bringing this one to my attention, rescuing it from the spam that I actually do discard.

SUBJECT: Re: I have found a weight loss product that really works.
TO: 4326858weighout
FROM: Jonathan Land <jland@incomplete.net>
DATE: 11/14/2001

My name is Linda Gillie. I am 31 years old. A mother of three, a wife of 13 years to a wonderful man, Michael My heart told me to share my story with you, so you don't give up hope. I have found a weight loss product that really works. It gets rid of fat fast and keeps it off, FOR GOOD! The youngest of 6 children, with both sides of my family prone to be he= avy, I have battled being overweight since I was a kid. I've been on ;just about every diet pro- gram, pill, liquid, & anything else you can think of. It was a never-ending cycle. Up, down, up, down, up. My weight loss and gain was a literal "yo-yo!" Nothing I did worked permanently! I had always gained back more than I would lose every time I got tired of a particular diet.

I was disgusted with my looks, mentally and physically depressed. I just about gave up hope forever of losing my excess pounds, until I was introduced to an all-natural weight loss product, which has changed my life in every way! My dearest friend and her husband have lost a lot of weight on a product called "Weigh Out". So, I decided to try it. In the first month I dropped from size 24 to 18 in 10 months I lost 78 pounds and 10 dress sizes and '85 I have kept it off for more than a year.

I'm so sorry to hear that because I'm casting people of your former descrip- tion for a movie!

My name is Jonathan Land, and I work for Sony Pictures. We're currently filming a remake of "Andy Warhol's Flesh for Frankenstein" helmed by hip, young filmmaker Spike Jonze of "Being John Malkovich" fame. And yes, it will be in 3-D. The new version is actually called "Spike Jonze's Andy Warhol's Flesh for Frankenstein," which any cult movie buff will get a jolly kick out of because Andy Warhol's now being credited twice for the same movie, which he probably never even saw so much as a poster for in the first place.

But hey, if he exploited his own good name, why can't we? I can almost hear him saying "ooooh, that's AW-ful" with his thin lips, barely making waves on his expressionless face, as his hand delicately flops forward on his wrist, as he sits in a booth in Studio 54, flanked by models of all genders.

Anyway, the point here is that the original movie was very gory, and they achieved this gore by the use of actual dead animal organs. Of course, it was disgusting, but it worked, and the rest is obscure film history. Unfortunately, the world is a much different place than it was in the 70s.

It's all for the best, anyway, since it's our obligation to the moviegoing to give them bigger and better entertainment, and therefore bigger and better real organs. That's why, in lieu of animals, we've decided to harvest the organs of fatally obese people. When I say fat, I mean orca fat. If I'm not going to have to hire a crane to lift them out of their house, it's not worth my time. And this will all come through on the silver screen. When a lung sits around the laboratory, it should sit AROUND the laboratory. You get the picture ... and if you do ... you GET the picture.

So since this weight-loss product has worked so well for you ... I'm sorry, but you're out of the running. HOWEVER, since you're sending this to a bunch of people, I was hoping that you could put me in touch with some of the people who purchase your product from you. Of course, I'm sure that "weigh out" works just fine, but I'm hoping that some people will get it and be too physically or emotionally sluggish to use it for a sustained period. Then we get them to sign the consent forms, ship them to a big-time Hollywood surgeon postmortem, and it's like Christmas in a carcass. Thanks in advance!

Ciao,

Jonathan Land

Casting Director

Sony Pictures

Author's Note: Spam donated by Hélène de Grosbois.

SUBJECT: Re: AFRAID OF CANCER
TO: dkoliadko
FROM: Jonathan Land <jland@incomplete.net>
DATE: 12/04/2001

AFRAID of CANCER??? And / Or Need Money?

Read the results of nine years of research by THE HOLLINGS CANCER INSTITUTE at The Medical University of South Caroline.

Go to: http://[URL deleted] click on products,then EllagiMax

After reading about EllagiMax,click onCoralMaxx another cancer fighter....then click on Oxy Plus, then Alo-Min

NO DRUGS..ALL NATURAL PRODUCTS!!!

For a few minutes of recorded testimonials call:

512-XXX-XXXX.

Afraid of cancer?

You bet, Mister! I've been afraid of cancer ever since the doctor told me I had it two weeks before I turned ten. *Cough*. For years and years my parents and I thought I had a Siamese twin attached to my head, but he never spoke or nothin' because he didn't have a mouth due to his lack of facial features, although one of his many bumps looked like it might have been a chin. So my daddy took a *cough* took a Sharpie pen he stole from a guy and gave my twin eyes, a mouth, and a sign saying "Kick him hard" on his back with an arrow pointing to me. Then we made him a wig out of my cat's hairballs. I named him Lumpy. And after I named the cat, I named my twin Jimmy. We live in a closet just like Harry Potter! One day I'm going to be as rich and famous as him. I know that kids who live in closets can make it! Look at Tom Cruise!

So one day Jimmy and I were looking out the window, watching TV though my neighbor's window. We don't have a TV, and we're not allowed to go outside because we're Mommy and Daddy's special secret. The neighbor mom was watching the cable repairman fix the TV, and we were watching this show on the Learning Channel all about cancer, then all of a sudden, they showed this thing called a tumor, which looked just like Jimmy *cough* without the Sharpie marks. Jimmy's dark secret was revealed, and there was an enemy among me.

I called up 911 as discreetly as I could without letting Jimmy know I knew he was really cancer, and help came right away. They brought me to a hospital and took good care of me *cough*. Jimmy was removed, and for my tenth birthday, I got him signed by the New York Yankees. There was even space left over to get the signatures of the *cough* Knicks, the *cough* Rangers, and Congress.

Unfortunately, when the police saved me from Jimmy, they also took my parents away. They're in jail now for child cruelty, and I'm in the hospital orphanage trying to raise money for my release. They won't let me go until I pay off my surgery, and they keep adding the daily boarding to my tab, so as the chief nurse says: "Oooh Honeychild, you are fucked, mmm, mmm, mmm, mmm, MMM." I'm supposed to be having chemotherapy, but I can't afford it, so at night I sleep next to the microwave. I set it for eight hours and nod off to the gentle hum. And you know what? I feel darn good in the morning! They keep telling me that I need real chemo because even though Jimmy's gone the cancer might not be gone, and if it gets let go for nine years like last time, I could grow a new Jimmy.

I really want to get out of here by Christmas ... I hope I get to see it *cough* this year. If you're the real deal, you're my ticket out of here and my key to being cancer free. I can't afford to buy your product to sell it and make money though. Please find it within your heart to send me a case. I'll make us both money, I will, I promise. I'll only take what I need and let the microwave work the rest of its healing magic.

I *cough* hope *cough* this works, Mister. I really need it. Please *cough*. Help.

Jonathan Land

✉

Author's Note: God forgive me for writing this on cold medicine.

....

SUBJECT: Re: Perfect Gift For Your Pastor or Church Secretary
TO: MinistryWare
FROM: Jonathan Land <jland@incomplete.net>
DATE: 12/12/2001

                    The Perfect Christmas Gift for your

                      Pastor or Church Secretary!!

Order now in plenty of time for Christmas!!

Wrestling with what to get your pastor for Christmas?‹ Give something that will truly assist him all year long!!

What about the poor church secretaries out there, that wrestle with figures for hours keeping track of the church's books, membership, and attendance?‹ Does anyone remember them on Christmas?

Church Management Software

MinistryWare Church Management Software will help either one or both of them be much more efficient.‹ Its simple Windows interface allows them to automate the procedures of managing church membership, tracking attendance, managing church expenses, tracking contributions and sending out year end reports, and much more.‹ They spend hours every week in paperwork.‹ MinistryWare can ease this burden for them and allow them to concentrate on other issues of taking care of their congregation.

Visit http://www.ministryware.com now to get more information and order.‹ You will have your copy in plenty of time for Christmas.‹

Keep your receipt as this purchase will be fully tax deductible as a religious contribution!!!

This year, give your Pastor or Church Secretary something that they can truly appreciate and use all year long!!!‹

> This is the perfect Christmas gift for a Pastor?
>
> Well, speaking as a Pastor, if one of my parishioners gave this to me, I'd kick them so hard in the rectory, their head would spin fast enough to make the little girl from "The Exorcist" ask, "What the hell's gotten into you?"
>
> You, my friend, haven't checked out the latest edition of the Non-Secular Sharper Image Catalog. The people who've made the PalmPilot and the VCR Co-Pilot have done it again with the God Co-Pilot! Your "MinistryWare" is just a stand-alone organizer. There's tons of software out on the market like that. It's as original and desirable as giving the gift of socks or life.

The God Co-Pilot is a PDA with a built-in cellular modem, GPS tracking system, and Taser. Most importantly, it comes with software called The KillFile. The KillFile uses the modem to sync up with servers containing The Database. The Database is the newest companion to The Bible. It's simple, direct, and compiled by God himself.

This is how it works: Updated once a minute, it conveniently sorts all living people into two categories . . . you guessed it, Good and Evil. If Person X winds up in the Evil list for three consecutive updates (as a black militant with a name like that just might), he'll get tossed into The KillFile. On the next modem sync, his name will be beamed down to the God Co-Pilot with the GPS coordinates closest to his Evil-doing self. Finally, he will have an "Act of God" delivered to him by the God Co-Pilot owner acting strictly as one of His messengers via the Taser set on "kill."

Sweet, huh? Now I bet you have a few questions, since this is all pretty involved, so I took the liberty of cutting and pasting the FAQ from their Web site for you:

Q: Isn't God a little more hands-off than this?

A: This isn't your parents' God. This is the new proactive God who's a lot more like Santa Claus but with higher stakes. Did you really think he was going to let all of this crazy shit go on for any longer? Come on!

Q: What gives me the right to carry out God's Will like this?

A: It's God's Will, jackass. Do what The Man says.

Q: How do I know that this is actually God's will?

A: God is a confirmed gadget buff. As a matter of fact, the CEO of God Co-Pilot LLC received this instant message upon the product's release: "Finally, someone got it right! I've been waiting for humanity to get to this point of technological development for ages. This is the greatest product ever. Knock 'em dead!"

Q: I preach in a small community in a tiny, rural, backwoods part of America that's still waiting for the arrival of cable TV. Will the modem get reception out here?

A: Good news, the modem is dual-band, so even if you're preaching in the boonies, you can still spread the Good Word.

Q: Won't this make me a religious fanatic?

A: Fuck no, buddy! It's all good. God just hates Evil. The thing costs $30,000 if you can afford that, or have someone give it to you. You're divinely blessed.

So there you have it. That's the God Co-Pilot, and if that's not the perfect Christmas gift for a Pastor, I don't know what is. Could I interest you in becoming a seller of this fine device?

Pastor Jonathan Land

....

SUBJECT: Re: Christmas Gift
TO: [Not a spammer . . . name withheld]
FROM: Jonathan Land <jland@incomplete.net>
DATE: 04/24/2002

I'm not sure what this letter was all about on the web. I was just following some links when looking for an article called, "The Perfect Pastor". I found the letter at:

http://thespamletters.com/letter.shtml?spamID=159&sortBy=d&start=0

I find it very difficult to accept this as anything close to "christian". The concept was cute, but the language found in the text was inexcusable. It was sickening.

Enough said.

Listen.

There are lots of horrible acts being committed in the world by many people. These acts are far worse than the language I use, and even what those words represent. People find my approach refreshing. As a matter of fact, I've been told that my "salty sermon" goes down quite nicely. The older folks appreciate my straightforward nature, and the kids think I'm hip, so they listen to me where most authority figures fail. If you tell a child that "drugs are bad," they will be curious and run to the nearest Rastafarian and begin their unholy experimentation. Now if you tell a child that "drugs are for jerkfaces," they won't go near the stuff, because they've been calling each other "jerkface" in the playground for years. They might not even know what it means . . . they just know that they don't want to be branded with the term.

My flock can reconcile my colorful vocabulary with my almost homoerotic, crazy fanboy love of God. I love God long time. I am a good man, and I do good deeds, and for that, I am rewarded by Him. Would God himself allow one of my parishioners to buy me a "No. #1 Pastor" T-shirt if such was not the case?

We need to be open about these things and speak naturally to one another, or we're no better than the Catholics. I'm sure they're staunchly against "obscenities" as well . . . on the surface. Yet behind closed doors, they're turning little boys into sexual pinatas. As disciplinarians they're only interested in ripping the astray new assholes so they've got more deviant options for their repression to be transformed into gratification!

I bet Islamic extremists have strict hang-ups about language, and look what they're capable of.

In America, we should be proud to use all of the great language God gave us. If you think that I am making the world a worse place by using it, so be it. All I know is that I've got the "No. #1 Pastor" T-shirt. What's in your closet?

Pastor Jonathan Land

....

SUBJECT: Re: Christmas Gift
TO: [Not a spammer . . . name withheld]
FROM: Jonathan Land <jland@incomplete.net>
DATE: 05/15/2002

It is so completely irrelevant what people think about your "hip" language. I realize you will say that it does not matter what I think either. You are correct. What matters more than anything else is, what does God think. I cannot believe God would be happy with an individual using language that is considered from the "gutter". Do we lower ourselves to the level of those we try to reach? How can a person get another person out of a hole if he is in the same hole? If God uses us to help others acheive heights in Him, we must first be at that height. You don't crawl in the hole, you throw them a rope. You sir, are not elevating anyone higher and closer to God with your foul language, you are lowering yourself. The only time it is recorded one of the desciples of Christ cursed was when he denied Jesus. All the justification you gave for your vulgar language was based on comparisons to other people. Why not compare with God? The Bible says if we compare ourselves among ourselves, we are not wise. Hhhhmmmm.

I'm not concerned with what is in your closet, but what is in your heart?

[Name Withheld]

My heart is filled with love. It swells with life's magnificent beauty, it aches to assist all souls in need, and it burns upon the rapid consumption of greasy foods.

You're making The Bible appear very cut-and-dry. Obviously such is not the case, since there are multiple interpretations out there, each one of which is championed by people who think their version is the one and only. The Good Book, as well as good books in general, and David Lynch's "Mulholland Drive" (a complex film worth watching if you can set aside the sinfully HOT lesbian scenes) are like that. While there are some base principles that can still be adhered to, a certain amount of looseness must be respected.

For instance, your equating of my foul language to being on the same level as "people in holes" strikes me as being a bit unrealistic. Do you truly believe that the foul language hole is the same as the murder hole or the promiscuity hole? Ha! "Promiscuity hole" . . . I'm going to have to use that one on Sunday.

I am on the ground floor, my friend. I'm in the yard, lying casually on the grass as He created me, basking in the sun's glorious rays as guided to Earth by His hand. The language I use is not a one-way ticket into the deepest, darkest, blackest pits of hell. It's an extension of my arm for which people can reach, grab on to, and allow me to pull them up with. I can't just sit there, hovering over the hole with my arm outstretched, telling them to jump for it. I am a compassionate human being, and if I have to stick my arm down in that hole to pull another human being up, than any dirt gathered upon it in the process is worth enduring. Is that not the right thing to do?

Pastor Jonathan Land

✉

SUBJECT: Re: Hydrogen Peroxide from producer
TO: Hydrogen Peroxide AS
FROM: Jonathan Land <jland@incomplete.net>
DATE: 01/23/2002

Dear Madam/Sir

Hydrogen Peroxide AS (HPAS) is leading producer of all concentrations of Hydrogen Peroxide at its state of art production facilities in Turkey. Our production capacity is 20 000 Tons per year on a 100% concentration basis.

If you can inform us of your requirements such as packing, quantity and any other commercial preferences we would like to offer you our competitive prices with the higest quality hydrogen peroxide.

If you would like to get further information about our company and products please visit our web site at: www.hydrogenperoxide-tr.com

Please do not hesitate to contact me through my mail : hguler

Ask HPAS hydrogen peroxide from your chemical importes/supplier

Sincerely yours.

H. GULEC

You, my friend, have made a very wise decision in contacting me, but I assume you must already know that, given who I am. Just in case you merely got lucky: The name's Jonathan Land, and I made headlines in newspapers all over the U.S. as the world's largest importer of hydrogen peroxide back in the 80s.

I manufactured "Imitation Swede" girls at my club, The Swede Den. Back then, people with a Swede tooth just loved the velvety-soft feel of Swede. Do you remember the Swedish Bikini Team from the Budweiser ads? Well, they were the Harlem Boys Choir before I got to them. That's an extreme example, but it was a challenge, and I'm proud we were able to pull it off. Our only other African-American male-to-Swedish female transformation was a member of the Jackson 5. He only went partially through the process and then had a change of heart. I dare not reveal his name because I don't want to take responsibility for the incomplete work.

Anyhoo, we pumped pure hydrogen peroxide through the mandatory thrice-daily showers, and we used Sharpie markers to make the future Swedes' eyes blue. It was so cute when they stumbled around. Unfortunately the business eventually failed because of the mental capacity of the girls who wanted to become Imitation Swedes in the first place. Most of the girls' idea of a Swedish accent is going "ya, ya, oh yaaaah" over and over. They forgot to capture the forlorn depression and emotional wear from binge drinking in "the dark months." Even though they were never advertised as anything more than "Swedishish," people were still let down by the lack of authenticity. The irony is that these girls came to California because they thought they could be actresses.

Fast-forward to today: I'm now on a mission. I founded the Church of Our Mistress of the Perpetual Blonde in Hollywood last year to make girls' dreams come true, or at the very least start them on a downward spiral that will thoroughly shatter their dreams once and for all. We take runaways and young actresses that can't find representation and give them everything they need to "make it" as a star. By "star" I mean Cinemax B-movie queen or stripper. We have a working partnership with Back Alley Bargain Breast Implants. The turnout of girls who lash out at their parents and/or can't get work has been phenomenal lately, and I and my staff can't turn them out as starlets fast enough.

Our blonding process (known as The Baptism) is essentially throwing a girl in a hydrogen peroxide-filled bathtub for three days with a snorkel and an IV, but there's currently a hydrogen peroxide shortage in California, and we've already drained all of the local drugstores. We've had a complete drought for a month. Right now we have about 300 girls with inch-long dark roots shivering in a corner of the basement, hiding in fear that they'll be seen and exposed as frauds. I bought them a few cans of yellow spray paint to tide them over, but they keep breaking their nails while trying to braid the hair like that.

So I can really use your service right about now. I'll need A LOT of the stuff. Approximately 500 gallons a month. I don't care how you send it to us. How much would that run me?

Father Figure Jonathan Land

Church of Our Mistress of the Perpetual Blonde

✉

Author's Note: Spam donated by Jeff Hobbs.

SUBJECT: Re: Are You a BOWLER? Check Out the HOTTEST NEW BOWLING BALL!
TO: joebowler
FROM: Jonathan Land <jland@incomplete.net>
DATE: 02/13/2002

How would you like to be the first in your bowling league to get your hands on the newest bowling ball from this innovative company? This new ball comes with a multi-density weight block with 800 grit sanded surface. This ball is so versatile, you can use it out of the box for heavy oil, or it can be shined to combat any condition. This ball has a very controlled break-point, which means higher scores and predictability.

Just some technical data for the serious bowler:

Radius of Gyration - Medium (2.530)

Differential - Medium (.050)

Hook Potential - 20 / 14 Dull/ Shiny on a scale of 1-20

Track Flare Potential - 6.5

Factory Finish Length - 6 on a scale of 1-10

Factory Finish Back-End - 8 on a scale of 1-10

Composition - Highly Reactive Urethane

Color - Lemon / Lime ....Very Attractive!

D-Scale - 76-78 Hardness

So if you would like some more information on this brand new product and want to be the envy of all your league bowlers, simply contact us at itstrikes and put "More Info Wanted" in the subject line and we will send along a website and some information about how to reserve yours today!

Hello,

I'd like to counter your proposition with another: How would YOU like to be the first in YOUR industry to get a piece of the newest innovative sport: Extreme Vertical Bowling.

We're looking for a manufacturer for league balls. These will have to be custom made to withstand several drops from approximately 10,000 feet in the air.

This is how it works in a nutshell: The bowlers will be outfitted with a ball and a parachute. For each frame, the bowlers are loaded onto a plane that climbs to 12,000 feet. Once the bowler jumps from the plane with ball in hand, they have 2,000 feet to release it, or they're "over the line." Then, and only then, are they allowed to pull the ripcord for their parachute. Repeat 10 times.

They'll be aiming at 10 pins secured vertically over a 4x4-foot target. The target itself will be made out of industrial strength Nerf, so the ball should be fine. However, depending on how far off target our bowlers are (aka throwing a "craterball"), the ball could be landing on a variety of surfaces.

Can you please let me know if such a ball is feasible?

Jonathan Land

CEO, Extreme Vertical Bowling, LLC

P.S. I know, what you're thinking ... you're thinking: "Can't people get hurt like this?" I mean, really, any sporting event can go haywire ... look at how many stray golf balls give folks concussions!

Author's Note: Spam donated by Mike Gammon and Cliff Vick . . . separately . . . it's not what you think.

....

SUBJECT: Re: New Pill makes your semen taste sweet-she'll swallow and love it
TO: 0sandmn0, 01bb932d.0fe13750
FROM: Jonathan Land <jland@incomplete.net>
DATE: 02/20/2002

Men, Do You Want to Increase the Amount of Oral Sex You Receive by 5 to 10 Times?

Now, Make Oral Sex a Treat . . . Instead of a Job!

SweetenZe is a new all herbal pill that can make your semen actually taste sweet.

No more salty or bitter taste. 98% of women say they would perform more oral sex and even swallow, if there partners semen tasted better.

Now with a single pill that makes you taste sweet, you can increase the amount of oral sex you receive by 10 times or more. Women all over the world are finally loving performing oral sex on there men.

There's nothing better than that intense feeling you get as your lover swallows every last drop. Try a bottle of SweetenZe if your not completely satisfied we'll refund 100% of your money. or Call 626-XXX-XXXX

This sounds like an interesting product, but it creates an intriguing dilemma for me.

I'm a highly disgruntled teenage employee of a Dunkin' Donuts in a location I probably shouldn't disclose. Even though it would appear that I have my whole life ahead of me, the present looks very bleak. I'm earning $5.50 an hour, working about 10 hours a week after school and on weekends selling donuts and coffee to a surly, unpleasant group of adults who should be laying off the high carbs. How these dangerously obese tight-asses gain such a thrill being nasty and mean while not allowing that to interfere with their passion for eating is beyond me. Long story short: I hate it here. Sure I could get another job, but with the hours I have to give being a high school student, it would just wind up being another fast food place because I'm not taking up elderly booty-wiping duty.

Of course, if my parents just gave me a reasonable allowance, which they can afford to do, I wouldn't have to waste my time in this doughy hell with these horrible, doughy people. Unfortunately my folks don't want me to be spoiled, and they're trying to show me the benefits of earning money. I can't say that I've learned that particular lesson. The only thing I have learned is that there is no such thing as satisfaction for a job well done when your job itself is completely unsatisfying.

So I'm stuck here. That, combined with the fact that I'm a 16-year-old virgin with a woody that just won't quit, and demoralizing acne that might as well spell out "kill me," tends to build up a little bile. For the last few months, I've been choosing to exorcise this bile, with a hefty side dish of semen, straight into the donut batter when no one's been looking.

Now, the donuts definitely taste funny according to a few customer complaints, so I'm undoubtedly going to be caught soon. If I could "sweeten the deal" with your product, that would totally rock, but I don't know if I'd get the same satisfaction out of doing it, even though I could probably get away with doing it for way longer. But what if they start liking the donuts more than they used to?

Sure they're still gobbling down my boys, but if there's no remote clue, like the current twinge of funk, it just isn't the same for me. I need to be able to think, "Yeah, take THAT, jerkoff!" and not be swarmed by a hungry mob, "Night of the Living Dead"-style, feasting for more of my sweat meat, chanting "mmmm . . . jizznuts . . . jiiiiizzznuuuutsss." This totally might backfire, causing my particular Dunkin' Donuts to become wildly popular, and forcing me into being overworked on my shitty salary!

So before I buy this stuff from you, I would need to know exactly what effect the outcome (and oh, do I mean out-come) might be in the donut batter. Would the donuts taste better than donuts with standard-issue semen, and worse than an untainted donut, or would such a heavenly delicacy be created that I could probably consider "going legit" and opening a franchise of my own, featuring my special secret ingredient?

Personally, I just can't wait to walk up to the sophomore I have an eye on and use the "Hey little girl, want to have some candy?" line when propositioning her.

Jon

Author's Note: Original spam donated by Iain Aitch.

....

SUBJECT: RE: The Stainless Steel Network
TO: The Sales Staff at BuyStainless
FROM: Jonathan Land <jland@incomplete.net>
DATE: 03/06/2002

Unsubscribe by clicking the link at the bottom of this E-mail! It's quick and painless.

The Stainless Steel Network is brought to you by

http://[URL deleted]

Stainless Steel PLATE For Sale!!!

Prime Material at a great discount Eastern European Made

$.66 FOB NJ

304L 1.125 x 60 x 240 5 Plates 23,651 .lbs

$.88 FOB GA

316L 1.125 x 60 x 144 1 Plate 2,985 .lbs

316L 1.750 x 60 x 287 1 Plate 8,792.lbs

316L 2.00 x 60 x 287 1 Plate 10,009.lbs

$.85 FOB TX

316L 2.00 x 60 x 144 12 Plates 60,301 .lbs

Stainless Slit Coil

75,000 .lbs Narrow Width 304 Coil Drops, various sizes, nice condition; Make Offer FOB Port of Philadelphia

Do you have a requirement for Stainless?

Ask us... We have the global resources to

get the job done right, for the right price.

I'm the new tour manager for a semi-obscure German "industrial music" group formerly named Einsturzende Neubauten. The name translates to "Collapsing New Buildings," so taking a cue from American heavy metal band, Basket Full of Puppies (nee Anthrax), they've changed their name to Flaumige Haschen ("Fluffy Bunnies"). It was a wise PR decision, even though they had the previous moniker for over 20 years. Their old fans will find the new name playfully ironic, and they really aren't gaining any new ones. Plus, it rolls off the tongue, which says a lot in a harsh language like German.

The band relies heavily on power tools and anything metallic that can be used as percussion for their live performances. Unfortunately road wear and tear plus many rainy outdoor festival gigs have compromised the equipment. We were in a pretty bad accident with the tour bus last year, and all of the decaying chainsaws, nails, drill bits, sheet metal, and touring personnel got tossed about like we were inside a blender, which is ironic, since the blender (along with the mixer and centrifuge) stayed put.

Everyone got cut up pretty bad, but with all of the screams and clanging, I'd say that it was hands-down their strongest performance in the time that I've been with them. It was pretty gruesome, though. I can only remember one sight as horrific, and that would be the backstage videotape of fellow German techno band Kraftwerk scootching across shag carpeting and shocking each other's naked asses with their fingers. I think they finally discovered something that was more fun to compute.

Anyway . . . Flaumige Haschen is a group of rough-and-tumble guys, and their multiple lacerations and severances didn't really bother them all that much. It was the ensuing lockjaw from the tetanus they all got from their rusty instruments that was very uncomfortable for them. Fortunately, having their jaws immobile in no way interfered with their vocal performances.

I just want to see that this doesn't happen again. We can afford better equipment. So to summarize: I have a very naive question . . . stainless steel doesn't rust, does it?

Jon

....

SUBJECT: RE: The Stainless Steel Network
TO: The Sales Staff at BuyStainless
FROM: Jonathan Land <jland@incomplete.net>
DATE: 03/06/2002

Jon,

Stainless doesn't rust. Hence "Stainless" :: Chuckles::

Mason

Cool. I wasn't sure if rust qualified as a stain. I thought it was more of a chemical reaction or an act of God. I'm a glorified roadie. I lack "book smarts," although I am smart enough to ask you this: If your name's Mason . . . why are you working in steel? Shouldn't you be in a more stone- or brick-oriented line of work? You probably get that a lot, don't you? I apologize.

Anyway . . . these guys are real whack jobs. Thankfully, I just tour with them when they're in the U.S. . . . I can't believe they've been shipping all of their crap over from Germany for all of these years. Whenever I pick them up from the airport, I just know that they've been disassembling the plane they came in on . . . probably by gnawing through it. Do you remember Animal from "The Muppet Show?" Imagine a band with 7 of him.

I've made a little progress with them on the expensive shipping front. On one of our days off the last time they were here, I took the boys to Home Depot. It was like Toys "R" Us to them. They ran around the place with hammers, and they literally banged out an album while they were there. Still, the band was disappointed with the quality of the sheet metal, so I'm still looking for some, which is why your mailing was well timed.

I realize, though, that you sell this stuff in large quantities, and while the boys would go nuts over owning a 10,000-pound piece of metal, I don't think it'll fit particularly well in the bus. And even if we can get it in there, I can't imagine that we'd be able to get up to a reasonable speed, or not crack the axles in half.

So do you sell smaller pieces, or is that not worth your company's time? If it's not, where might I get just a couple of little slabs of stainless steel? I just know I'm going to get this stuff, and then they're going to tell me it's out of tune.

Jon

....

SUBJECT: RE: The Stainless Steel Network
TO: The Sales Staff at BuyStainless
FROM: Jonathan Land <jland@incomplete.net>
DATE: 03/13/2002

Jon,

I appreciate your sense of humor.

Thanks. It's mostly a defense mechanism from working with this group. My grandfather always used to say to me, "If you ever meet a German, keep them laughing, and they'll become close with you." Of course, the saying ended in "then you shiv the bastard in the back when he least expects it." Gramps was a World War II vet, and he never quite reacclimated to a more tolerant world afterward.

What is the name of the band?

Einsturzende Neubauten is the former name. Flaumige Haschen is the new one. They haven't released anything under the post 9-11 name yet. Here's a link to their bio on http://ubl.com:

http://ubl.artistdirect.com/music/artist/bio/0,,426945,00.html?artist= Einsturzende+Neubauten

Anyway, I can sell you any amount BIG OR SMALL. We accept CREDIT CARDS. Let me know EXACTLY WHAT SIZE YOU WANT, AS WELL AS WHAT YOU WANT IT TO SOUND LIKE.

I need:Thickness x Width x Length.

Jeez, if memory serves, the old plates were about 4 feet wide, 2 feet long, and about 2 inches thick. I'd need 3 of them. As for what they sounded like . . . they sounded like a whole lot of clanging noise to me. I'll have to fire off a discreet note to one of their producers about what they expect from metal, so I'll have to get back to you about that. I can't believe I'm actually inquiring about this. It's embarrassing. I've got to look into a gig tour managing a folk singer or something like that. Someone sulky with an acoustic guitar.

I know the details aren't fleshed out yet, but do you have any sort of ballpark figure or range about how much this might run, given the info above?

If you want ROUND BARS, I need to Know Diameter and LENGTH.

Based on your sound and pitch and reverb needs etc etc.... I can take an edu-cated (more educated than someone not involved in metals... like you!!!) As to which grade you need!

OK, I'll contact the producer soon. I'm having a stroke of genius though . . . do you guys make steel drums, or is that something totally different from what you do? Maybe if I just order those instead and surprise the group with them, they'll go for it. I haven't seen that many steel drum band concerts, but I don't think it's possible to play one of those things wrong. I think it would be great to see them pounding away at the things with their usual fiery intensity only to produce soothing Calypso music. Then I could book them on cruise lines instead of the standard crappy venues that only willfully obscure bands like them can get gigs at.

Maybe they could even become successful, or at the very least tolerable! Who am I kidding; they'll just set the things on fire and leave me holding the bag when the club owner gets mad. Okay, scratch the steel drum thing. Just let me know the ballpark for the slabs. Thanks.

Must . . . get . . . out . . . while . . . alive . . .

Jon

CHAPTER 8
Foreign Affairs: Part 2
Nigerian Scam Artists

⌧

The easiest and most satisfying spammers to bait are the Nigerian con men. You can tell them anything no matter how absurd, and they'll respond because they truly believe that they'll eventually get your money. Need proof? Read on!

⌧

Author's Note: Thanks to Joshua S. Freeman for gracing me with this gem. There's nothing more I want from life now than to have this person respond to me.

SUBJECT: Re: ASSISTANCE
TO: Raymond Etiebet
FROM: Jonathan Land <jland@incomplete.net>
DATE: 07/03/2001

HON. RAYMOND ETIEBET(DR).

ATTN: Joshua S. Freeman,

DEAR SIR

REQUEST FOR URGENT BUSINESS RELATIONSHIP

FIRST, I MUST SOLICIT YOUR CONFIDENCE IN THIS TRANSACTION. THIS IS VIRTURE OF IT'S NATURE AS BEING UTTERLY CONFIDENTIAL AND TOP SECRET.

WE ARE TOP OFFICIALS OF THE FEDERAL GOVERNMENT OF NIGERIA CONTRACT REVIEW PANEL WHO ARE INTERESTED IN IMPORTATION OF GOODS INTO OUR COUNTRY AND INVEST- ING IN EUROPE WITH FUNDS WHICH ARE PRESENTLY TRAPPED IN NIGERIA.

IN ORDER TO COMMENCE THIS BUSINESS WE SOLICIT YOUR ASSISTANTANCE, KNOWLEDGE AND EXPERTISE TO ENABLE US RECIEVE THE SAID TRAPPED FUNDS ABROAD, FOR THE SUB- SEQUENT PURCHASE AND INVENTORY OF THE GOODS TO BE IMPORTED AND THE INVESTMENT IN EUROPE.

THE SOURCE OF THIS FUND IS AS FOLLOWS: DURING THE PREVIOUS MILITARY REGIMES IN OUR COUNTRY, GOVERNMENT OFFICIALS SET UP COMPANIES AND AWARDED THEMSELVES CONTRACTS WHICH WERE GROSSLY OVER-INVOICED IN VARIOUS MINISTRIES. THE NEW CIVILIAN GOVERNMENT NOW SETUP A CONTRACT REVIEW PANEL WHICH I AND MY COL- LEAGUES ARE MEMBERS AND WE HAVE IDENTIFIED A LOT OF INFLATED SUM, DUE TO OUR POSITION AS CIVIL SERVANTS AND MEMBERS OF THIS PANEL, WE CANNOT AQUIRE THIS MONEY IN OUR NAMES. I HAVE THEREFORE, BEEN DELEGATED AS A MATTER OF TRUST BY MY COLLEAGUES OF THE PANEL TO LOOK FOR AN OVERSEA PATNER INTO WHOSE ACCOUNT THE SUM OF US$31,000 000,00 (THIRTY-ONE MILLION UNITED STATES DOLLARS) WILL BE PAID BY TELEGRAPHIC TRANSFER. HENCE WE ARE WRITTING YOU THIS LETER.

WE HAVE AGREED TO SHARE THE MONEY THUS:

1. 70% FOR US (THE OFFICIALS)

2. 20% FOR THE FOREIGN PATNER(YOU)

3. 10% TO BE USED IN SETTLING TAXATION AND LOCAL AND FOREIGN EXPENSES.

IT IS THIS 70% THAT WE WISH TO COMMENCE THE IMPORTATION BUSINESS AND THE
INVESTMENT IN EUROPE. PLEASE NOTE THAT THIS TRANSACTION IS 100% SAFE AND WE
HOPE THAT THE FUNDS CAN ARRIVE YOUR ACCOUNT IN LATEST TEN(10) BANKING DAYS
FROM THE DATE OF RECIEPT OF THE FOLLOWING INFORMATION . A SUITABLE COMPANY
NAME AND BANK ACCOUNT(COMPANY OR PERSONEL) INTO WHICH THE FUNDS CAN BE PAID.

THE ABOVE INFORMATION WILL ENABLE US WRITE LETTERS OF CLAIM AND JOB DESCRIP-
TION RESPECTIVELY. THIS WAY WE WILL USE YOUR COMPANY'S NAME TO APPLY FOR
PAYMENTS AND RE-AWARD THE CONTRACT TO YOUR COMPANY NAME.

WE ARE LOOKING FOWARD TO DOING BUSINESS WITH YOU AND SOLICIT YOUR CONFIDENTI-
ALITY IN THIS TRANSACTION.

PLEASE ACKNOWLEDGE RECIEPT OF THIS LETTER USING THIS E-MAIL ADDRESS. I WILL
BRING YOU INTO THE COMPLETE PICTURE OF THIS PENDING PROJECT WHEN I HAVE HEARD
FROM YOU.

YOURS FATHFULLY,

HON. RAYMOND ETIEBET(DR).

--- "Joshua S. Freeman" wrote:

Raymond,

I own many companies and corporate accounts. Which one, in particular, did
you have in mind in terms of doing this business transaction together?

Where did you get my e-mail address?

Best wishes,

Joshua

DEAR JOSHUA S. FREEMAN,

THANK YOU VERY MUCH FOR YOUR RESPONSE. MY COLLEAGUES AND I ARE OVERJOYED BY
YOUR RESPONSE AND YOUR APPARENT UNDERSTANDING OF THE NEED FOR CONFIDENTIALITY
IN ALL MATTERS RELATING TO THIS TRANSACTION,WE GOT YOUR E-MAIL ADDRESS FROM
A COLLEAGUE FORMERLY WORKING IN THE NIGERIAN CHAMBERS OF TRADE AND COMMERCE
WE DO NOT KNOW IF HE KNOWS YOU PERSONALLY OR WHERE HE GOT YOUR E-MAIL ADDRESS
FROM BECAUSE WE DID NOT ASK HIM TOO MANY QUESTIONS SO THAT HE DOES NOT START
ASKING US QUESTIONS ALSO, IN FACT HE DOES NOT EVEN KNOW THAT WE HAVE CONTACTED
YOU AND WE DO NOT INTEND GIVING HIM ANY FEEDBACK SO AS YOUR CONFIDENTIALITY
IS WELL PROTECTED. WE HAVE DECIDED TO MOVE FORWARD WITH YOU. PLEASE FIND THE
DETAILS BELOW.

THE MONEY IN QUESTION (US$31,000,000,00) IS AS A RESULT OF AN OVER INVOICED
CONTRACT PAYMENT WHICH THE ORIGINAL CONTRACTOR HAS BEEN PAID HIS TOTAL ENTI-
TLEMENT LEAVING THE OVER-INVOICED AMOUNT(US$31,000,000,00) IN A CODED ACCOUNT

AT THE CENTRAL BANK OF NIGERIA(C.B.N). WE, BY VIRTURE OF OUR POSITION AS THE CONTRACT REVIEW PANEL AND BEING THAT WE ARE THE ONLY ONES AWARE OF EXISTENCE OF THE FUNDS, WE WANT TO AQUIRE THE FUNDS FOR OURSELVES. TO DO THIS IT BECOMES EXTREMLY NECESSARY FOR US TO OFFICIALIZE THE PROCESS OF FUNDS TRANSFER MAKING IT TAKE THE SEMBLANCE OF AN ACTUAL CONTRACT PAYMENT. THIS WHERE WE NEED YOUR ASSISTANCE.

THE CONTRACT WOULD BE PERCIEVED TO HAVE BEEN EXECUTED BY YOUR COMPANY FOR THE NIGERIAN NATIONAL PETROLEUM CORPORATION(NNPC), WHICH IS THE FEDERAL STATUTORY CORPORATION FOR WHICH THE ORIGINAL CONTRACT WAS DONE, WHILE ITÌS VERY NATURE AS AN ORGANISED DEAL, REMAINS WITHIN OUR(PARTNERS ONLY EXCLUSIVE KNOWLEDGE.)

WHAT MUST BE DONE:

YOU ARE TO RE-TYPE AND FILL IN THE ACCOMPANYING DETAILS INTO YOUR LETTERHEAD AND INVOICE PAPERS RESPECTIVELY, SIGN THEM AND SEND THEM BACK TO ME BY FAX IMMIEDIATELY, TO ENABLE ME MAKE APPLICATION FOR THE FUNDS TRANSFER TO THE CEN-TRAL BANK OF NIGERIA THROUGH MY OFFICE THE CONTRACT REVIEW PANEL. WE WILL HAVE A NOTARY PUBLIC ENDORSE THE FAX COPY, SO IT CAN SERVE AS AN ORIGINAL. YOUR COMPANY SHALL BE INTRODUCED BY US AS THE BONA FIDE CONTRACTOR AT THE NIGERIAN NATIONAL PETROLEUM CORPORATION(NNPC) AS WHO EXECUTED CONTRACT NO:043/NNPC/WR-PH/93. BASED ON THE HOMEWORK WE HAVE DONE, THE APPLICATION WILL BE APPROVED AND SENT TO THE CENTRAL BANK OF NIGERIA(CBN) FOR THE FINAL APPROVAL AFTER WHICH THE FUNDS WOULD BE TRANSFERED TO YOUR NOMINATED ACCOUNT BY TELEGRAPHIC TRANSFER OR SOLAR DRAFT FOR US ALL.IN RESPECT TO YOUR QUESTION ON THE ACCOUNT TO USE WE JUST NEED A GOOD ACCOUNT THAT CAN RECEIVE THIS MONEY.

WE BEING CIVIL SERVANTS ARE VERY CONSCIOUS OF THE DICTATES OF THE LAW, THIS IS IN ORDER TO SAFE GUARD OUR POSITIONS AS CIVIL SERVANTS AND ALSO THE LEGAL INTERESTS OF YOUR COMPANY NOW AND IN THE FUTURE, FOR THIS WE WOULD MAKE SURE YOUR COMPANY IS REGISTERED WITH THE NIGERIAN PETROLEUM CORPORATION(N.N.P.C) AS A CATEGORY "A" CONTRACTOR BECAUSE ONLY A BONA FIDE REGISTERED COMPANY IS GRANTED CONTRACTS.

ONCE THE APPROVAL OF THE FEDERAL MINISTRY OF FINANCE IS READY, FOREIGN CON-TRACTORS AMENDMENT ACT OF 1995 PROVIDES THAT THE BENEFICIARY OF THE CONTRACT PAYMENT(YOU) SHALL BE REQUIRED TO BE PRESENT IN NIGERIA AND ENDORSE THE CLASSIFIED TRANSFER DOCUMENTS AT THE INTERNATIONAL REMITTANCE OFFICE OF THE CENTRAL BANK (C.B.N). ALTERNATIVELY IF THE BENEFICIARY IS UNABLE TO COME TO NIGERIA TO ENDORSE, HE IS LIABLE TO RETAIN THE SERVICES OF A LOCAL ATTORNEY WHO IS A REGISTERED CONSULTANT AT THE CETRAL BANK OF NIGERIA, TO ENDORSE ON HIS BEHALF PROVIDED THERE IS A PROPERLY EXECUTED POWER OF AUTHORITY TO THAT EFFECT. I WOULD ADVISE THAT IN YOUR RESPONSE YOU SHOULD INDICATE THE OPTION MOST SUITABLE TO YOU.

I WANT TO EMPHASIZE HERE THAT ALL EXPENSES INCURED BY ALL PARTNERS IN THE PRO-CESS OF THIS TRANSACTION SHALL BE PAID BACK WHEN THE FUNDS ARE REMITTED. THE FUNDS SHALL BE SHARED IN THE RATIO 70% FOR US 20% FOR YOU AND THE REMAINING

10% FOR REFUNDING ALL EXPENSES INCURED BY ALL PARTIES DURING THE COURSE OF THIS TRANSACTION.

AT THE END OF THE TRANSACTION TWO OF US SHALL ARRIVE THE COUNTRY OF YOUR NOMINATED BANK ACCOUNT FOR THE PURPOSE OF SECURING OUR SHARE AND USING YOUR ASSISTANCE TO PURCHASE GOODS FOR IMPORTATION TO NIGERIA. WE INTEND TO IMPORT AGRICULTURAL MACHINERY AND APPLIANCES OR COMPUTERS AND ACCESSORIES.

PLEASE YOU CALL ME OR FAX ME IMMEDIATELY YOU HAVE READ THIS. I WAIT IN EARNEST ANTICIPATION OF YOUR RESPONSE.

BEST REGARDS

HON. RAYMOND ETIEBET (DR.)

N.B YOU CAN CALL ME AT ANY TIME OR VERY LATE AT NIGHT NIGERIAN TIME BY THEN MOST PEOPLE WILL BE ASLEEP AND THE TELEPHONE LINES WILL BE LESS BUSY.YOU SHOULD ALSO SEND ME YOUR PRIVATE AND CONFIDENTIAL AND FAX NUMBERS

RETYPE INTO YOUR LETTER HEAD

THE DIRECTOR GENERAL

ENGINEERING AND PROJECTS

NIGERIAN NATIONAL PETROLEUM CORPORATION

FALOMO-IKOYI

LAGOS NIGERIA.

DEAR SIR,

COULD YOU KINDLY USE YOUR GOOD OFFICE TO ACT IN FAVOUR OF OUR BILL WHICH HAS BEEN PESENTED TO YOU.

DUE TO YOUR DELAY IN ACTING ON OUR BILL, WE ARE NOW CONTINUALLY BEING HARRASSED BY OUR CREDITORS.

SO, KINDLY PAY OUR FUNDS INTO OUR ACCOUNT BELOW BY SWIFT TELEGRAPHIC TRANSFER.

BANK NAME: ==============================

ADDRESS: ==============================

PHONE: ==============================

ACCOUNT NO: ==============================

BENEFICIARY: ==============================

YOURS SINCERELY,

SIGN, STAMP,DATE.

RETYPE IN YOUR INVOICE

THE DIRECTOR GENERAL

ENGINEERING & PROJECTS

NIGERIAN NATIONAL PETROLEUM CORPORATION

FALOMO-IKOYI

LAGOS NIGERIA.

DEAR SIR,

BELOW IS THE BILL OF OUR CONTRACT NO.043/NNPC/WR-PH/93 WHICH HAS EARLIER BEEN PRESENTED FOR YOUR NECESSARY ACTION AND APPROVAL››››

››››››››››››››› S/N ITEMS AMOUNT

1.FLUSHING & CALIBRATION OF THE IKOT-EKPENE UYO AXIAL STATION

$18,640,000.00

2.LAYING OF FLOW PIPES FROM WARRI TO PORT HARCOURT

$8,000,000.00

3.REPAIR OF FACULTY TURBINE AT THE BONNY HABOUR

$4,360,000.00

TOTAL

$31,000,000.00

YOURS SINCERELY,

STAMP,SIGN,DATE

Dear Nigerian Ambassador,

My name is Jonathan Land, and I'm a distant relative of a man you've contacted recently named Joshua S. Freeman. When I say "distant relative," I don't mean that I'm one of his siblings or offspring that barely acknowledges his impaired but continuing existence through yearly birthday phone calls and more infrequent visits; I'm just a cousin more times removed than I'd like to bother to calculate. More importantly, I have the power of attorney over Mr. Freeman's estate . . . unlike Mr. Freeman himself.

The reason I have total control over Mr. Freeman's finances is because he's screwier than a pimp recruiting station at a job fair, and unfortunately you have seen what it's like to personally deal with him. What I'm trying to say here is that not only does his elevator fall a few stories short of the belfry, but no matter how you get up there, you're bound to be hip deep in guano.

One time he even donated money to Parkinson's research, which, on a good day, is a shaky proposition at best. I figured he must have seen an ad for it with their new pitchman, because he kept on talking about helping out "that poor Alex Keaton boy." His nursing staff and I were very impressed with the powers of association he hasn't displayed in months, but we knew it was only a fleeting thing. If I may be so bold as to describe your country as being on some sort of American cultural delay, I just made a reference to a television sitcom called "Family Ties," but it might be lost on you. If Nigeria's anything like England, it's probably going to be debuting there any month now. Does that make sense, or do I need to explain what a television is? For all I know, you could have sent this e-mail through a Kinko's hundreds of miles away from you via telegraph.

Anyhoo, I've been away for the past week, in which time it would appear that Mr. Freeman himself struck up a conversation with you, first inquiring about a deal you presented to him, and then ultimately refusing it. Please ignore that correspondence completely, and I apologize for the inconvenience. How he figured out the password to his e-mail account is beyond me, but I've already changed it to "password," which he would never get in a million years. Please deal directly with me from here on at the address you are receiving this e-mail from.

To recap: You solicited Mr. Freeman to help you in a financial matter that would require him to register one of his company's bank accounts with the Nigerian Petroleum Corporation to hold a sum of money that would later be redistributed in the form of a 70%, 20%, 10% split, apportioned between you, Mr. Freeman, and transaction expenses.

We are, in fact, VERY interested in this opportunity, and I do have the power to make it a reality. There is one stipulation, though. Since we would be doing you a great service, I think 20% of the kitty is a little skimpy.

However, we do not want more money! We would like property in key locations around Nigeria to open up a chain of stores. We would also need the proper business licenses for said chain, as well as translators to help us implement everything. If this is possible, I'll fill you in on the nature of the business, but like your deal, it too is confidential, and I'd rather not divulge any pertinent info until it's a go.

Thank you, and I hope I can repair our wounded relationship and start anew on the right foot . . . unless you guys have some cultural stigma in regards to feet or the right-hand side of the body.

I'm looking forward to your reply, and I'm very eager to make this happen.

Thanks again,

Jonathan Land

Power of Attorney for Joshua Freeman

⊠

Author's Note: It would appear that the sender of this e-mail address was turned in to some authority before I could get to them, because this e-mail bounced; the sender was kicked off of their ISP.

That's such a shame. I was itching to describe the stores I was going to open called "I Can't Believe It's Not," a chain. These fantastic stores would allow you to put down payments on things that don't exist but should, like teleporters, robot butlers, and pleasant-tasting sugar substitutes. E-mail me at <jland@incomplete.net> if you'd like to invest!

SUBJECT: Re: URGENT RESPONSE
TO: Raymond Etiebet
FROM: Jonathan Land <jland@incomplete.net>
DATE: 07/09/2001

DEAR JONATHAN,

THANK YOU VERY MUCH FOR YOU E-MAIL, MAY BE YOU ARE GODSENT, MY PARTNERS AND MYSELF, WE HAVING DIFFICULTIES LOOKING FOR A SUITABLE PARTNER SINCE YOUR UNCLE REFUSED OUR PROPOSAL. YOUR ASSURANCE THAT YOU CAN HANDLE ON HIS BEHALF IS VERY ENCOURAGING AND I PRAY THAT WITH YOU WE HAVE FOUND A PARTNER COMMITTED TO THIS PROJECT AS WE ARE.

I am as committed to this project as Mr. Freeman is now committed to the Timeless Dignity Nursing Home. Yeah, I felt bad about it at first. I finally got my little girl potty trained after 12 years (we all do things in our own time), and I couldn't bear to take any more of that sort of crap. Ethically I was questioning whether it was right to incarcerate him, but fuck it; he doesn't know me from the cardboard cutout of me that I leave around to make him think I visit him more than I do. So he's well taken care of, and I can cruise around Florida in my Chrysler Sebring convertible searching for a new mommy for my little girl.

Actually, that makes me wonder . . . what's your mail-order bride industry like? I assure you, I do not discriminate against ANYONE. I would fully incorporate my bride-for-hire into my life in the customary American fashion. We'll take long walks on the beach together, she'll prepare and later clean up our candlelight dinners, and she'll have lots of my babies while

she hangs out and maintains the property. I wouldn't be "buying a woman";
I would be putting an investment into a wife that I will grow to love and
respect as soon as I possibly can.

WE WILL NEED YOU TO RETYPE DETAILS (AN APPLICATION FOR PAYMENT AND AN INVOICE
TO THE AMOUNT OF 31MILLION USD) WHICH I WILL SEND TO YOU ALONG WITH THIS
EMAIL, INTO THE RELEVANT LETTERHEADED AND INVOICE PAPERS IT IS THESE THAT WE
WILL USE TO APPLY FOR RELEASE OF THE FUNDS INTO THE NOMINATED ACCOUNT WHICH
YOU WILL INCLUDE IN THE REQUESTED PAPERS. WHEN WE RECEIVE THE APPLICATION AND
INVOICE WE SHALL PROCEED TO FILE THEM IN THE RELEVANT MINISTRIES AND PARASTAT-
ALS IN THE MEAN TIME WE WILL REGISTER AND INCORPORATE A COMPANY IN NIGERIA
WITH THE NAME THAT APPEARS ON THE LETTERHEADED WHICH YOU WILL SEND TO ME. WE
HAVE ALREADY MADE ALL THE NECCESSARY ARRANGEMENTS AND CONNECTIONS TO ENSURE
THAT YOUR APPLICATION FOR PAYMENT WILL BE APPROVED VERY FAST WITHOUT MUCH
SCRUITING AND ENABLE THE FUNDS BY RELEASE. ONCE PAYMENT HAS BEEN APPROVED ALL
THAT IS LEFT IS THE ENDORSEMENT (SIGNING) OF THE INTERNATIONAL REMITTANCE DOC-
UMENTS TO EFFECT THE TRANSFER OF THE FUNDS TO YOUR ACCOUNT.

I just faxed the info. Let me know that you got it okay.

IT IS GOOD THAT YOU ARE SATISFIED WITH THE SHARING RATIO AND AS REGARDS THE
INVESTMENT IN NIGERIA IT IS A WONDERFUL IDEA IN WHICH WE ARE HIGHLY INTERESTED
IN PARTICIPATING BECAUSE NIGERIA IS PRESENTLY WIDE OPEN VIRGIN COUNTRY, VERY
OPEN FOR BUSINESS INVESTMENT COUPLED WITH HUGE POTENTIAL FOR GROWTH.

Let's get technical here. I want to open a chain of stores. What do I need to
do to get the ball rolling? Do I need to submit a business proposal, get per-
mits, licenses, bribe unions, what??? And how can you help me? Can I just
tell you what I want here, and you can tell me if you think it'll fly, and just take
care of all the details for me? I guess that would work best for me.

Look, I've put myself (and, of course, Mr. Freeman's estate) in a vulnerable
position here! Don't make me make it difficult for you to get your money out
of my account! I can take or leave the money. I don't need the money. I want
to be a clever entrepreneur. I want to be hip and trendy and at least 5 years
ahead of my time. (By the way, that's 5 American years of hipness, which
from my brief research translates to about 50 Nigerian years of hipness.)

My stores will be the biggest thing to hit Nigeria since . . . I'm sorry, I don't
know enough about Nigeria to know what's the most recent popular thing; I
just know it's tragically unhip. No offense.

Jonathan Land

P.S. I hear Nigeria is a lot like Utah. Is that true?

N.B YOU CAN CALL ME AT ANY TIME OR VERY LATE AT NIGHT NIGERIAN TIME BY THEN MOST PEOPLE WILL BE ASLEEP AND THE TELEPHONE LINES WILL BE LESS BUSY.YOU SHOULD ALSO SEND ME YOUR PRIVATE AND CONFIDENTIAL AND FAX NUMBERS

RETYPE INTO YOUR LETTER HEAD

THE DIRECTOR GENERAL

ENGINEERING AND PROJECTS

NIGERIAN NATIONAL PETROLEUM CORPORATION

FALOMO-IKOYI LAGOS NIGERIA.

✉

SUBJECT: Re: URGENT ASSISTANCE
TO: IBRAHIM.ISA.MOMODU
FROM: Jonathan Land <jland@incomplete.net>
DATE: 07/16/2001

IBRAHIM ISA MOMODU

FAX: 234-1-XXXXXXX

LAGOS - NIGERIA

Sir,

REQUEST FOR URGENT BUSINESS RELATIONSHIP

First, I must start by soliciting your confidence in this transaction. This is by virtue of its nature as being utterly confidential. I want to count opn your confidence and ability to prosecute a transaction of great magnitude involving a pending business transaction requiring utmost secrecy.

We are top officials of the Federal Government Contract review Panel(CRP) who are interested in importation of goods into our country with fundswhich are presently trapped in Nigeria. In order to commence this businesswe solicit your assistance to enable us transfer some trapped funds intoyour account.

The source of this fund is as follows: In the past few years, the Federal Government of Nigeria allocated funds to its Ministries and Agenciesbased on their requests for funds for the execution of projects. Due to the Government's Central Accounting System, all such allocated funds werepaid into the Central Bank of Nigeria, which is the apex bank as well as the banker to the Federal Government. The federal government Governmentof Nigeria therefore set up a Contract review Panel(CRP) with a view to identifying duly

completed projects, unutilized funds and make recommendations as appropriate. We have identified a lot of the unutilized funds and we want to transfer
some of it abroad. However, by virtueof our position as civil servants and
members of this Panel, we cannot acquirethis money in our names. I have therefore been mandated, as a matter of trustby my colleagues in the Panel, to
look for an overseas partner into whose account we would transfer the sum of
US$24,500,000.00 (Twenty Four Million, Five Hundred Thousand US Dollars).

After the transfer, we have agreed to share the money thus; 25% for the
account owner (you), 70% for us (the officials) and 5% to be used forthe reim-
bursement of taxation and all local and foreign expenses. It isfrom our 70%
that we wish to commence the importation business. Please notethat this transaction is 100% safe and we hope to complete the transfer latestin ten (10)
banking days from the date of receipt of the information below.

We urgently require the following from you by fax;

1. Name of Beneficiary (account owner), telephone and fax numbers foreasy communication.

2. Name and Full Address of Company.

3. Complete particulars of the Bank where you wish the funds to be transferred. This should include the bank address, account number, the telephone
and fax numbers of the bank.

The above information will enable us write letters of claim and job description respectively. An application for payment will be made infavour of the
beneficiary (you or your company) and the funds shall be transferred to the
bank and account number specified in the application.

We are looking forward to doing business with you and please treat this transaction as strictly confidential. Acknowledge the receipt of thismail using the
above Fax number or email.

Thanks for your anticipated cooperation.

Yours faithfully,

IBRAHIM ISA MOMODU

Dear Mr. Momodu,

By any chance, do you know a member of the Nigerian Federal Government
Contract Review Panel by the name of Raymond Etiebet? I was conducting
a very similar deal with him on behalf of a relative named Joshua Freeman,
a man who's been so affected by age and medication that he makes
Ronald Reagan seem as coherent and lively as . . . well, anyone who can

blink without drooling. Unfortunately, my last e-mail to him seems to have bounced back.

Since you're both part of the same team, I was wondering if you could pass me his new contact info, unless you'd like to work out a better deal with me. My loyalty is completely malleable when touched by the golden hammer of wealth.

Dr. Jonathan Land

Power of Attorney for Joshua Freeman

✉

Author's Note: Spam contributed by Hélène de Grosbois.

....

SUBJECT: Re: REQUEST FOR ASSISTANCE
TO: hamza kalu
FROM: Jonathan Land <jland@incomplete.net>
DATE: 07/16/2001

OFFICE OF THE CO-ORDINATOR,

CONTRACT REVIEW PANEL,

NIGERIAN NATIONAL PETROLEUM CORPORATION(NNPC).

DR HAMZA KALU, FAX: 234 1 XXXXXXX

ATTN: Jonathan Land,

REQUEST FOR ASSISTANCE-STRICTLY CONFIDENTIAL›

I AM DR HAMZA KALU, THE CO-ORDINATOR OF THE FEDERAL GOVERNMENT OF NIGERIA CONTRACT REVIEW PANEL OF THE NIGERIAN NATIONAL PETROLEUM CORPORATION(NNPC).› SOMETIME AGO, A CONTRACT WAS AWARDED TO A CONGLOMERATE OF FOREIGN COMPANIES BY MY COMMITTEE ON BEHALF OF (NNPC),THE CONTRACT WAS OVER INVOICED TO THE TUNE OF US$24.5 MILLION. THIS WAS DONE DELIBERATELY, THE OVER INVOICING WAS A DEAL BY MEMBERS OF MY COMMITTEE TO BENEFIT FROM THE PROJECT, WE NOW DESIRE TO TRANS-FER THIS MONEY WHICH IS PRESENTLY IN A SUSPENSE ACCOUNT OF THE NNPC IN THE DEBT RECONCILIATION COMMITEE(DRC) INTO AN OVERSEAS ACCOUNT WHICH WE EXPECT YOU TOPROVIDEFOR US.

Dr. Kalu,

I'd be more than happy to help . . . but I've recently received another offer like this that gave me a 30% cut of even more money. You bump my share up to 35%, and I'm your man.

Dr. Jonathan Land

P.S. I see that you're a doctor. I'm a doctor too! I'm just curious, what was your field of study, or are you a real Ph.D. doctor like me?

. . . .

SUBJECT: Re: THINKING ABOUT IT
TO: hamza kalu
FROM: Jonathan Land <jland@incomplete.net>
DATE: 07/16/2001

Dr. Jonathan Land,

I recieve your email.About your request,i will discuss with my partners,and get to you later.

Excellent! I look forward to hearing the result of the discussion.

I own a doctorate degree in civil engineering,how about you?
Dr. Hamza Kalu.

I didn't buy my degree as you point out above. I am a medical doctor. I specialize in veterinary medicine, but I dabble in optometry. I'm actually in the middle of developing an alternative to LASIK surgery, involving a laser pointer, a magnifying glass, and a steady hand. It's great; you can even do it at home! You might want to buy a box of rats to try it on before you raise the glass to your kids.

Dr. Jonathan Land

SUBJECT: Re: CALL ME
TO: hamza kalu
FROM: Jonathan Land <jland@incomplete.net>
DATE: 07/16/2001

Dr. Land,

My partners have reclined your offer simply for the reason that you are
already dealing with somebody else, and by the way is the transaction same
with ours, that is does it originate from my country please let me have more
information then we can talk better , give me your number I promidse to call.

Dr. Hamza.

Dr. Hamza,

If you've "reclined" my offer, then why are you asking me for more info?
That's not what someone in a reclining position would do. They're usually out
on a beach with a fruit drink or in front of the television with a six-pack.

Who should I be dealing with? Who's the chief muckity-muck, the top dog,
the head cheese? Can't we buck the system here? Maybe you and I can work
out a little something. Point of clarification: While I'm sure you're a handsome
man, I meant "work out a little something" purely financially with no sexual
overtones. I'm saying you could get a cut of my cut, and that's not a circumcision reference. If you want a circumcision reference, call Dr. Schwartz in New
York. He does babies of all ages, but (a) you'd have to come to America, (b)
that's probably not covered by your health insurance, and (c) if it ain't broke,
don't fix it.

Listen, don't feel awkward about pissing off your coworkers. I'm a bidness-
man, I speak the language of bidness, and if you speak the language better
than anyone else, and we can communicate well, then the bidness I'll do, I'll
do with you.

I am a desirable suitor. As a mafia friend once told me, if you want to make
an omelet, you've got to break some legs. Of course, when he originally said
it, it just came out as one long uber-syllabic word, and I didn't decipher it for
about a week and a half.

I'll give you my phone number, but I'd much rather have all of our dealings in writing, (1) so I can have a written record of our dealings for my accountant, and (2) so I can include them in my eventual memoirs. Once I'm famous and wealthy, I plan on putting out a book of letters showing the path to exactly how I became famous and wealthy, and I'm certainly hoping that you'll be a large part of my getting there.

My phone number is: (xxx) xxx-xxxx

Dr. Land

....

SUBJECT: Re: CALL ME
TO: hamza kalu
FROM: Jonathan Land <jland@incomplete.net>
DATE: 07/16/2001

Dr. Jonathan Land,

Call me on my private phone 234 1 XXXXXXX, i would really like to meet you on phone.

Dr. Hamza Kalu.

Call Nigeria? I just checked with my long distance provider, and I get no deals whatsoever calling your neck of the woods. For the price of a 5-minute call to Nigeria, I can get an hour with a "pro" AND a hotel room (albeit on the bad side of town). Not that I'd need more than 5 minutes, of course.

I think we're getting to know each other just fine through this wonderful free medium of the Internet.

Any word on your and your partners' decision?

Dr. Jonathan Land

SUBJECT: Re: act fast.
TO: hamza kalu
FROM: Jonathan Land <jland@incomplete.net>
DATE: 07/23/2001

Your first message:

Jonathan,

Send down the information i requested for so i can begin making preparations
with the apropriate quarters, as it is when i get hold of the information i
will proceed to register you as a contractor with the corprate affairs commis-
sion here and then with the NNPC. Certificates will be issued to this regards
and be aware that certificates that the certificates will be backdated to suit
the contracts dates, i will tell you here that this wil cost us areasonable
amount of money but we have it all penciled down so you have to be totally
commited to this transaction. Once i make the registration and the certificates are issued i shall send them to you as you will be needing them. After
this i will then forward an application on your behalf as you will be the
front man for the release of the money into an account you will provide, hence
the reason i am in haste cause the earlier we begin the earlier we conclude
and reap the benefits What i need are. Your full names and address to use as
the beneficiary, this should be the same name with the account holder,

Tel and fax no, where i can direct all correspondence to.

Banking information. i.e. bank account, bank name, address, anything neccessary for the transfer. I await the information. Note that we can not proceed
without this information.

Hamza.

Your second message:

Jonathan,

Why the delay, i am axiously waiting to begin this transaction proper. Please
act fast so we can proceed, and please if you are dealing with us deal with us
only as we do not wan someone with divided attention.

Hamza.

Dr. Impatient,

1) I want this to happen as quickly as you do. I apologize for being out of town for 2 days on a bidness trip with my ISP being down. I'll make sure to sit right in front of my computer, checking my e-mail every minute on the minute until I get your response from this e-mail and reply immediately. Please note I'll be out from 6 to 8 p.m. at a "black-tie" function.

2) You have NEVER answered my question about the 35% . . . Whaazzzupwitdat? If you want my undivided attention, you are simply going to have to pay for it. Yes, I do have another individual courting me for my bidness . . . that's how we do it in America, and the prize goes to the highest bidder. Believe me, dealing with the emotional roller coaster you bring to the table is not pleasant for me, and my other suitor appears to be more stable. Unfortunately, you seem to be the one who's willing to offer a larger cut. Hopefully you'll use some of the cash you'll get from this transaction to get some professional help.

Now that I think of it, I'd like that worked into the contract. I'm starting to worry about you, Hamza. If you just want to talk about stuff, I'm here for you. I mean that.

So what's with the money???

Dr. Land

. . . .

SUBJECT: Re: CALL ME
TO: hamza kalu
FROM: Jonathan Land <jland@incomplete.net>
DATE: 07/23/2001

Jonathan,

What do you take me for a fool or something, my friend get serious or stop sending me mails.

Hamza.

I'm perfectly serious, even though I prefer a humorous tone for my correspondence. Is that so wrong? If you want me to tone it down, I'll tone it down, even though the last time I went down tone, it was late at night and I got mugged. SEE . . . FUNNY!!! You love it! Some of my best friends refer to me as "the broke man's Groucho Marx."

Okay, okay, I'll cut it out. How can I make amends?

Dr. Jonathan Land

....

SUBJECT: Re: REALISE THE REALITY
TO: Raymond Etiebet
FROM: Joshua S. Freeman <jfreeman@incomplete.net>
DATE: 07/23/2001

Dear J. Freeman,

How are you, your work and family? Thank you for your response on the mail sent to you about a month ago, and I want you to know the reality on this transaction, this is not a matter of joke, I and my colleagues were overjoyed with your first response, but along the line you dissappointed us, well it is confidential matter, if you know you have interest on this transaction you can still get back to me through this same box, and if not get back to me as well so that we will be able to look for another interested person that can take good care of this.

Best Regards

Hon. Raymond Etiebet

Hello, Mr. Etiebet,

I am in quite excellent spirits, but I'm afraid I don't know exactly what you're talking about. Can you please fill me in? I'm getting a sneaking suspicion that my secretary, Mr. Land, has been meddling in my affairs while I was in Paris looking for the proper model to donate some of her eggs to me.

I'm afraid I'll be forced to give Mr. Land a tongue lashing he won't soon forget, although I'm reluctant to use that term, given his fondness for smearing his naked body with Alpo and liberating all of the dogs in the local kennel for what he likes to call his "woof-woof, licky-licky bath." Honestly, good help is SO hard to find. Sane help is even harder to come by.

So what's been going on? What are we supposed to be in the middle of here?

Joshua S. Freeman

SUBJECT: Re: REALISE THE REALITY
TO: Raymond Etiebet
FROM: Jonathan Land <jland@incomplete.net>
DATE: 07/23/2001

Dear J. Freeman,

How are you, your work and family? Thank you for your response on the mail
sent to you about a month ago, and I want you to know the reality on this
transaction, this is not a matter of joke, I and my colleagues were overjoyed
with your first response, but along the line you dissappointed us, well it is
confidential matter, if you know you have interest on this transaction you can
still get back to me through this same box, and if not get back to me as well
so that we will be able to look for another interested person that can take
good care of this.

Best Regards

Hon. Raymond Etiebet

Your Honor,

I do not appreciate (a) being snubbed in the middle of a transaction, and
(b) having my explicit orders ignored! All transactions dealing with Mr.
Freeman go through me. Me being ME, not me being HIM! I've told you
before and I'll tell you again right now: Mr. Freeman has the cognitive capacity of a cauliflower ear, the rational reasoning of a radish, the beleaguered
brain function of a broccoli tree . . . do you understand yet, or am I going
to have to draw you stick-figure art similar to what I provide Mr. Freeman
with, explaining dense concepts like the art of breathing and the difference
between sleep and death?

You're on probation, Mr. Etiebet . . . I want to continue this transaction, but I'm
sincerely doubting your ability to handle it properly!!! Get your head in the
game!

Do you want to make this happen or not?

Jonathan Land

Power of Attorney for Mr. Freeman

SUBJECT: Re: send info
TO: hamza kalu
FROM: Jonathan Land <jland@incomplete.net>
DATE: 07/30/2001

Dr Jonathan Land,

i recieved your email.It seem that you are not serious about the
transaction,anyway i have met with my partners and we have concluded to
offer you 31% of the funds,if you are intrested we should proceed with the
transaction immdiately because we have less than a week for the money to be
transfered to your account.So send the information we requested for if you are
interested and if you are not you should let me know.

Dr Hamza.

The percentage of my net gain in a project is directly proportional to the
percentage of my attention I give to it. Now that you've upped the ante to
31%, you've just bought yourself a new and improved Jonathan Land compared to the 25% version you were previously dealing with. I will be exactly
6% more serious than before! As a token of my goodwill, I will ensure that
this correspondence will contain 6% fewer jokes.

By my calculations, since my ex-wife recently relieved me of 50% of my net
worth, with half of that being earmarked for the support of my 5 ex-children,
that means that I now take you more seriously than my ex-wife and any
given one of my ex-kids. Does that put things in perspective for you?

Do you understand exactly how seriously I'm taking you now? I've given you
a precise quantitative value . . . what more do you want?

Ah yes, you want my bank info. Here we go:

Bank Name and address:

Yodelehhehoo

91 Lederhosen Lane

Umlaut, 8023 Zurich

Account number: F4K3-5UM83R

OK . . . let's party,

Dr. Jonathan Land

P.S. That's my Swiss bank account info . . . is that okay, or do you need an
American bank?

Author's Note: The phone and fax numbers given are for the U.S. Secret Service Nigerian scam division. They never called me back, so hopefully Mr. Kalu will just turn himself in. I don't have time for this . . . I am a busy, busy man.

SUBJECT: Re: not complete
TO: hamza kalu
FROM: Jonathan Land <jland@incomplete.net>
DATE: 07/30/2001

Jonathan Land,

At least we are making progress but the information is still not complete, we need a beficiary name to the account, your tel and fax number for this will be included in the application.

Here we go!

Name on the account: Ima Fakir (sister-in-law)

Tel: 202-406-8000

Fax: 202-647-3000

Do you not feel that an account in the US will be more apropriate that is if you have one of course, where i believe we are realy farmiliar with the banking procedures taxes and everyother thing. The eyes of the government of my country are too much on swiss banks, so i hope you understand why i will feel more comfortable with a bank in america.

I hear that Swiss banks have lots of holes in them. Most agencies look right through them. Plus, I have a lot more money in the Swiss account, so the amount to be deposited will probably go unnoticed. The only bank I trust in America is the Nobel Sperm Bank. If I forget my ATM card and I need quick cash, I stop by there, drop my load, and hit the road. They pay well. My most recent trip there took care of braces for 3 of my kids. There are other benefits too: they used my sperm to make that Haley Joel Osment kid. I'm the biological father of an Oscar nominee! I'm what's known as "high-class ass" over there.

Seriously, the Swiss (post-WWII) have never done me or my family wrong.

Please do send down the remaining information, in this order.

Your full names and address, your tell and fax number, I believe you are the beneficiary to the account hence we need the full names and address.And then your phone number i can be reaching you on.

I expect your reply so that i can proceed with the registration and submission of the application.

We should be good to go here.

Jon

....

SUBJECT: Re: Act fast.
TO: hamza kalu
FROM: Jonathan Land <jland@incomplete.net>
DATE: 07/30/2001

Dr. Jonathan Land,

Your quick response is needed for us to complete this transaction on time. Using your words you promised to be 6% more serious but you are still showing the same attitude, you do not respond to my mails on time. I told you earlier there is a lot to be done concerning this transaction, the earlier we begin the earlier we conclude.

Send the information and let's begin.

Dr. Hamza.

Okay, I just sent you the info.

I wish you'd be a bit more relaxed. I AM being 6% more serious, but if you'd like me to be 3% less serious so I could be 3% more timely, I will do that for you. Just say the word.

Dr. Jonathan Land

P.S. My ass hurts and I have no idea why.

SUBJECT: Re: Act fast.
TO: hamza kalu
FROM: Jonathan Land <jland@incomplete.net>
DATE: 07/30/2001

Dr. Jonathan Land,

Thanks for the response, but you still left out your full address, as this
will reflect in the application were are making, with this in mind to avoid
further delay i took the liberty of securing the application forms for the
release of the funds into your account. I am sending a specimen of this forms,
please fill and send back to me.

Dr. Hamza.

Okay, I'll have my accountant check these out on Monday, and I'll send them
out then.

I'm getting all excited and tingly, but that has nothing to do with my ass hurting as I mentioned before.

Jon

P.S. My ass no longer hurts; thanks for asking. I don't know why I bothered
saying that. Clearly if you don't have common courtesy, you're incapable of
feeling the guilt that I'm trying to manipulate out of you. Why do I even try,
Hamza, why?

✉

SUBJECT: Re: joint partnership venture
TO: zuma sankoh
FROM: Jonathan Land <jland@incomplete.net>
DATE: 07/30/2001

On Tue, 24 Jul 2001, zuma sankoh wrote:

I am Sankoh Zuma-Azeez,brother of detained Fondah Sankoh from Sierra
Leone,there is a war going on in my country and so my family members escaped

to Senegal while I am presently in Ghana in the statues of a refugee monitoring events. Because of the present crises,my environment is not conducive for investment and more over,most of my brother's properties and account have been frozen by the present government of Tejan Kabbah.

Now, I want to set up a business overseas and I have $50 Million United State Dollars set aside for this project, I decided to contact you to help me in setting up a business, but would not want my name or family name to be used.

I am prepared to give you a certain percentage of the total sum if you can assist me in claiming this funds after I most have transferred it out of Ghana through the help of a friend who is a diplomat with ECOWAS(Economic Community of Wesr African States) to Europe.

Please, do contact me immediately for further details.As soon as I hear from you, and confirm your willingness to assist I will set in motion the movement of the money from Ghana to Europe and all relevant documents will be handed over to you as the familyÎs foreign partner.

Best regards,

SANKOH ZUMA-AZEEZ

Joshua S. Freeman wrote:

Hi Zuma,

Sure, I'll be happy to help. I'm forwarding this email to my business manager, Jonathan.

He has access to all my accounts and holdings and can manage this project without involvement.

I'm sure you'll enjoy working with him.

best wishes,

Joshua

Hello,

I'd like to introduce myself. I'm Mr. Freeman's business manager. He forwarded me the correspondence above. I have final say on all financial dealings here because his daddy didn't like how he was blowing his allowance on strippers and coke.

I'm also a veteran of 'Nam, and I've got an ear necklace that Marlon Brando could use as a belt. I say fuck the money, let's you and me go get your brother back. I've got enough guns and rocket launchers to take on all of those guerrilla fuckheads. I was going to go over and take care of the whole thing myself over the weekend, but if you'd like to be my ammo caddy, I'd appreciate it.

Also, please send me a picture of your brother so I know the one guy in the country besides you not to kill.

Let's reunite your family,

Jonathan Land, Esq.

P.S. Sankoh ... is your family responsible for that shitty coffee substitute?

....

SUBJECT: Re: REALISE THE REALITY
TO: Raymond Etiebet
FROM: Jonathan Land <jland@incomplete.net>
DATE: 07/30/2001

Mr Jona,

Thank you for your response, which one are you?

I am the "bad boy." My collaborators are known as "the cute one," "the shy one," "the one dating Britney Spears," and "the one boinking the cute one."

Which one are you?

I don't know what is wrong with you it seem as if you are not very serious about this matter, or do you think am here for fun, if am to deal with plants or flowers I would have go to the normal routine, look this transaction is what I and my colleagues relies on for our future purpose, as you know we are just an ordinary civil servants on a public figure is as if the money coming in for us is as much, but we need to survive, why can't you just think and reason with me, we are in need of your assistance on this transaction for both of us to be able to realise something at the end of the day.

Would you believe that you're the second Nigerian government official to ask me about my level of gravity toward a financial situation today? I don't know what it is about me that makes people think I'm not a serious guy, but I am as serious as your average student film, and when I'm being sincere, I'm as serious as a sideways suppository.

Seriously, I'm down with the plan, Stan. What's the next step?

Please, let me know what you are on to, and let me know your mind instead of one thing to be Two things at a time.

I find your proverbs as fascinating as they are unfathomable. Chalk it up to cultural differences. Anyhoo, I am a very dedicated person. As a matter of fact, if I were to listen to the women in my life, I bet every one of them would affirm for you that I have a one-track mind.

Am waiting for your urgent response.
Hon Raymond Etiebet

Done! Where do we go from here?

Jon

....

SUBJECT: Re: confidentaility
TO: hamza kalu
FROM: Jonathan Land <jland@incomplete.net>
DATE: 08/08/2001

Dr. Jonathan,

I am waiting,but for confidentaility sake do it yourself and send it on time.

Dr.Hamza.

Dr. Hamza Kalu,

I'm afraid I have some bad news. I have been hired by your boss to evaluate the performance of you and your peers. Most of the folks running the same operation have greatly outperformed you, delivering the goods from the stupid Americans for admirable amounts of money. While Raymond Etiebet has made Employee of the Month, I'm going to have to ask you for your res-ignation. Please try to contain your jealousy when you pass his cubicle or it's into the tiger cage with you. I don't want to rub it in, but you should see his parking space. You could even fit a Cadillac in it. I will be kind enough to write you a recommendation:

> Dear Jackass,
>
> I wouldn't count on Hamza Kalu to secure any amount of money from so much as an outdoor fountain. If you're seriously considering hiring him, you don't deserve to stay in business.
>
> Thank God he's off of my hands,
>
> Dr. Jonathan Land

We're looking for deal closers here, not chitchatters. During our lengthy exchange, I hosed you like a firefighter. If I kept this going, I am 99% sure I could have gotten you to brand my name on your ass. I'm withholding the 1% on the off chance that you might do it yourself for some reason.

Not only did you not bring home the bacon, but you left yourself vulnerable by (a) continually writing from a traceable computer that has now apparently been pointed out to the FTC, and (b) enclosing some of our bogus documents for the fake American. These are exactly the sort of things that can be used against you, when handed over to the authorities. So, to teach you a lesson, I've handed all of the material to the authorities to use against you. As I see it, you no longer work for us, so hanging you out to dry is merely a vindictive pleasure I get as an auditor.

Buh bye! I've counted all of the office supplies, so don't even bother.

Dr. Jonathan Land

....

SUBJECT: Re: confidentaility
TO: hamza kalu
FROM: Jonathan Land <jland@incomplete.net>
DATE: 08/08/2001

Dr. Jonathan Land,

I know from the beigining that you are not a consistent businessman,you don't know what's up you are noisemaker.STOP writing me because i am a busy man.›

Dr. Hamza Kalu.

I'm sorry to take you away from the people who actually fall for your scam.

I kid, I kid!

Seriously, what other info did you need from me? Let's go forward with this thing, blah, blah, blah, etc. I want to be rich and so forth. How can I mend our strained relationship. I'm totally serious now, yada, yada, yada.

Dr. Land

....

SUBJECT: Re: confidentaility
TO: hamza kalu
FROM: Jonathan Land <jland@incomplete.net>
DATE: 08/08/2001

Jonathan Land,

If you disturb me again i will use african vodoo agaainst you. You will loose your manhood and may die infact i am looking at you now from a calabash of water and wondering if i should strike you dead but i see a girl an innocent girl, her spirit is strong i will let you pass this time.

Hamza.

Hamza,

You're the funniest fucker in the world. I'd like to see your African Voodoo against my American Technology. I'm a top muckity-muck in the Department of Defense. I'll have a Smart Bomb in your lap faster than you can play Hot Potato with it. They'll be picking those voodoo pins out of the remnants of your ass right up until the funeral.

So seriously, I'm not a cop or anything:

a) Are you even remotely near Nigeria?

b) How many people do you send e-mails like this out to, and how many actually fall for it?

c) Why did you keep writing back to me when I was obviously yanking you harder than a wood chipper? I could imagine that you deal with a lot of humorless folks in this line of work, and I might be a breath of fresh air.

Essentially, I'm really curious: how well has this racket worked for you?

According to http://home.rica.net/alphae/419coal/ the scam you're running is actually a major industry in Nigeria, so I guess it's going well.

Jon

✉

Author's Note: Spam donated by Bobby Allen.

SUBJECT: Re: URGENT ASSISTANCE
TO: Audu Bello
FROM: Jonathan Land <jland@incomplete.net>
DATE: 10/03/2001

----- Original Message -----

From: "Audu Bello"

To:

Sent: Friday, September 28, 2001 9:13 PM

Subject: URGENT ASSISTANCE

Dr Audu Bello

Director, ProjectImplementation

Falomo office

complex Ikoyi Lagos.

e-mail:du_bellad

STRICTLY CONFIDENTIAL

Sir,

It is my great pleasure in writing you this letter on behalf of myself and my colleagues. Your particulars were given to me by a member of the Nigerian Investment Promotion Council (N.I.P.C) who was at the Federal Government Delegation to your country during a trade exhibition. I have decided to seek a confidential cooperation with you in the execution of the deal described hereunder for the benefit of all parties and hope you will keep it as a top secret because of the nature of this business.

Within the Ministry of Petroleum Resources where I work as a Director,Project Implementation and with the cooperation of Four other top officials,we have in our possession as overdue payment bills totalling TwentyEight Million, Six Hundred Thousand U.S Dollars (US$28,600,000.00) which we want to transfer abroad with assistance and cooperation of a foreign company and/or individual to receive the said fund on our behalf or a reliable foreign non company account to receive such fund.

The amount represented some percentage of the total contract value executed on behalf of my Ministry by a foreign contracting firm which we the officers over invoiced. Though the actual contract cost have been paid to the original contractor, leaving the balance in the tune of the said amount which we have in principles gotten approval to remit by Telegraphic Transfer (T.T.) to any foreign bank account you will provide. Since the present Government of Nigeria is determined to pay every Foreign Contractor all debts owed so as to maintain good relationship with Foreign Government and Government Financial Agencies, we have decided to include our bills for approvals with the cooperation of some officials from the Federal Ministry of Finance (F.M.F) and the Central Bank of Nigeria (C.B.N).

We are seeking your assistance in providing a good company's account or any other offshore bank account into which we can remit this money by acting as our main partner and trustee or acting as the original contractor. This we can do by swapping of account and changing of beneficiary and other forms of documentation upon application for claim to reflect the payment and approvals to be secured on behalf of our company. This processes being internal arrangement with the departments concerned.

I have the authority of my partners involved to propose that should you be willing to assist us in the transaction your share of the sum will be 30% of the US$28.6Million, 60% for us and 10% for taxation and miscellaneous expenses.

The business itself is 100% safe, provided you treat it with utmost secrecy and confidentiality. Also your area of specialization is not a hindrance to the successful execution of this transaction. I have reposed my confidence in you and hope that you will not disappoint me.

(nigerian time) Monday to friday.

Awaiting your anticipated cooperation.

Yours' faithfully

Dr Audu Bello.

```
------------------------
```

Dr. Bello -

I am pleased by your decision to place such trust in me, but I am puzzled
by your e-mail. The To: address showed turner@trading.u-net.com, but the e-
mail was delivered to my account BUSies@coastalnet.com. If your message was
intended for someone else, please disregard my reply. I also see that your e-
mail was sent from an IP address belonging to an ISP in California, and I am
concerned as to how you will be able to conduct Nigerian government business
from that location. If it was meant for me, I must place some conditions on my
participation in your plan. Since I am a highly visible public figure, I am
unable to participate directly.

I would ask that you address all communications through my trusted agent
and assistant, Dr. Jonathan Land, CPA, BMF. jland@incomplete.net. Dr. Land
has power of attorney for all of my affairs, and he handles all of my business transactions. As an act of good faith on your part, I must ask that you
deposit one percent (1%) of my 30% of the $28.6 million into my PayPal account
via online transaction. I have already made arrangements for the deposit of
$85,800 into that account, and Dr. Land can provide the detailed procedures
for your deposit. Surely, one percent of my 30 percent is not too much to ask
in order to confirm your sincerity.

Looking forward to doing business with you (though you should not correspond
with me directly).

Mr. B.U. Sies, HMFIC

Hello Dr. Bello, you Nigerian Fellow!

I'm the aforementioned Dr. Jonathan Land, and I will be conducting Mr. Sies's
business. Like metal and virgin men, I conduct my business fast, so if you
diddle around on my watch, you will lose my ear, which you can't afford.
I see from my recent audit of Mr. Sies's finances you have yet to deposit
the 1% into his PayPal account. Please do so if you wish to continue this
transaction.

Another point of note: I don't know if you keep up with world events, but
from what my underlings tell me, there has been a massive terrorist attack
in New York City that has caused much death and destruction, and several
charities have been established to deal with whatever has to be dealt with. I
don't know the details. I like to keep myself sheltered from the news so I can
remain objective in all situations. Some people call it "blissful ignorance,"
but I call it "la la la fluffy bunnies fluffy bunnies" after the loud phrase my

personal assistant utters while she sticks her thumbs in my ears and covers my eyes when something I shouldn't see comes on the television or radio.

Mr. Sies is a prominent, wealthy man. His staff is currently attempting to change his appearance from philanderer to philanthropist. Here's the point: I'm paid on retainer, and I have nothing to gain from this transaction, but I'm willing to put up 10% of Mr. Sies's 30% if you're willing to put up 20% of your 70% for one or more of the charities dealing with these tragic events.

What do you say, my good man? Are we ready to do business?

Dr. Land

....

SUBJECT: Re: URGENT
TO: Audu Bello
FROM: Jonathan Land <jland@incomplete.net>
DATE: 10/03/2001

Dear Dr Land,

Thanks for your email, this transaction has to follow stages of proper docu-mentations.Kindly furnish me with your private Phone/fax number for easier communication.

Endeavor to call me unfailingly upon reception of this mail on my direct tel number 234-1-XXXXXXX for further details/dsicussions.

While i await to hear from you my warm regards to you and your family.

best regards,

Dr Audu Bello.

Phone? Fax? Are you joking? The Sies family has a centuries-old feud with the Bell family and refuses to use any telephone-derived product. As an employee of Mr. Sies, I have followed suit. And just before you start to be a wiseass, I'm on a cable modem! I don't think you do your research well at all. What's next, are you going to crack wise about crack? I'm very jumpy about that, especially since I'm still a frequent user of the stuff, but either you knew that or you were planning on feigning stupidity!

I just checked Mr. Sies's account again, and you have yet to make a deposit. I'm going to enclose a picture that my child drew of me, and I want you to look at it and tell me if you think I'm the type of person you'd like to fuck with.

I don't believe you're serious about doing business with me. You insult me, my employer, his intelligence, and my personal assistant's intelligence, since she's the one who writes all of my correspondence for me. (Assistant's Note: It's true!) I'm the beauty, she's the brains. (Assistant's Note: I'm cute too. I'm just not his type!)

So are you serious or not? (Assistant's Note: I love him when he's mad . . . *sigh*.)

Dr. Land

....

SUBJECT: Re: URGENT
TO: Audu Bello
FROM: Jonathan Land <jland@incomplete.net>
DATE: 10/11/2001

----- Original Message -----

From: "Audu Bello"

To: "B. U. Siesat"

Sent: Sunday, October 07, 2001 4:08 PM

Subject: URGENT

I am very puzzled by your representative attitude he is not taking the trans-action serious i would love to deal directly with you. Kindly furnish me with your phone/fax number for easier communication. Awaiting your urgent response.

best regards,

Dr Audu Bello.

Perhaps my agent's attitude is because of your failure to respond to our request for an act of good faith on your part. I notice that there has been no change in my PayPal account to indicate that you have made any deposit. Trust me, you don't want to piss him off (or his very cute assistant, for that matter)!

You cannot deal directly with me, as I am currently dedicating nearly every hour that I'm awake to production and delivery of armaments for the U.S. Military to allow the sustained bombing of Afghanistan to continue. If you need to fax documents to me, you can fax them to (202) 406-8000. Please include a voice number where my agents there can contact you. My personal phone number is classified, and all calls are recorded (a matter of national security).

B.U.Sies

Dr. Audu Bello,

You have pissed me off beyond my wildest imagination. I know this for a fact, because I have put a lot of thought into what scenario would fill me with the most possible anger. Well, the Emmys have been postponed once again. I turned red with rage and cursed like a sailor, which is as bad as it gets for me. I immediately enrolled myself in an anger management course.

I didn't even have the opportunity to attend my first class when I was sent your letter from Mr. Sies. Your questions of my intent and sincerity drove me totally bonkers, especially given the fact that YOU are the one who is not dealing with me seriously or with the respect and timid cowering I'm accustomed to. When I read your letter, I violently slammed my hand down on the table, startling my poor assistant to the point that she jumped in my lap! (Assistant's Note: He totally startled me, stirring deep emotions of passion and longing within. The lap thing was a good move, huh? I think I felt something move!)

Dr. Bello, I assure you that I can't be any more serious about this transaction. You have money, and my client has a bank account that is no stranger to the transfer of large amounts of funds, so we seem very well suited to one another. (Assistant's Note: Dr. Land's a Libra and I'm a Taurus, so we seem very well suited to one another. *sigh*.) I'm taking this as seriously as I can, given that I'm dealing with a party of the first part (you) who's a total fruitcake, and please, feel free to take offense at that.

What's the holdup with the PayPal deposit? Do I need to send my assistant over there to show you how to do it? (Assistant's Note: COOL! Hey, do you have a monarchy over there? I've always wanted to be a princess! Would it be taboo to have your royalty married to a white chick? I'm so cute though ... and bubbly, you'll love me, and I can wave like a pro! :) :))

I assure you that I'm totally serious here, and I'm eager to begin this transaction on behalf of Mr. Sies. Please stop wasting my valuable time and let's do this! (Assistant's Note: My God, he's irresistible! I need to sit on his lap again. Maybe I should throw out all of the other chairs in the office.)

Dr. Land

(Assistant's Note: Hey, I have access to all of Dr. Land's (and therefore Mr. Sies's) files and account info. I would do anything, and I mean anything, for Dr. Land. If you are in fact not happy dealing with him, you can deal directly with me at jenny@incomplete.net, and hopefully we can get everything done in a way to make all parties happy! As much as seeing him mad is a turn on, I think if I can pull this deal off for him, I'll score major points.)

....

SUBJECT: A Fantastic Proposal
TO: abhht, kannpc, alabo5, alhaji_suleimanabubakar, alhaji_suleimanabubakar
FROM: Jonathan Land <jland@incomplete.net>
DATE: 07/08/2002

Dear Illegitimate Nigerian Businessmen,

I have a proposition for you, please hear me out.

My name is Jonathan Land. I'm a former Secret Service agent who used to spend a significant amount of time investigating your "419" scam. Frankly, running around after you guys is tedious and confusing, like trying to get a book of replies to spam published. So if I can't beat you, I'll join you. Man, did I want to beat you, though, with the biggest government-issue billy club I could still lift.

I realize how much money is to be made in your little endeavor. A sucker used to be born every minute, but due to gross overpopulation, new statistics show that there's a sucker born every 3.9 seconds, according to the May 2001 issue of the "Barnum Report of Monetary Advantage." That's a lot of suckers to be had.

I'm contacting the lot of you because you guys are at the top of your fraud, the cream of the crap, the golden dregs at the bottom of the barrel of bobos. Plus, I've used my connections to investigate all of your criminal records, and you've all come out clean. Congrats ... you're all very good at what you do.

Unfortunately, what you do is under intense scrutiny, and people around the world are becoming privy to the fact that you've been running a con as long as a marathon. So the game has to change in order for you to keep playing, and I'm the guy that can help ... for a fee, of course.

I've seen your lengthy convoluted missives a thousand times over. If it's not about a political statement, it's about abandoned money, or a business transaction gone awry. Whatever it is ... it's too detailed and too much to deal with for your average e-mail fool. Why do you think television's so popular? Thinking's out; staring glassy-eyed is in!

You've got to go straight for the heart ... the heart that's already bleeding. I'm talking about charity here ... from the people who give little kids coins on Halloween for UNICEF to corporations who donate millions of dollars to the causes they see fit or that are in vogue.

What you need to do ... all of you ... is to join forces and create a bogus organization that fights "the scammers" that are giving places like Nigeria a bad name in the world's view. The more the "419" scam becomes popular, and the higher you raise your profile, the more money your new organization, that publicly combats "these people," will make. Has your sense of irony walked off hand in hand with your sense of human decency? Get with it, people. You sit there and rake it in for a few years, and then you all cash out and lead a life of criminal leisure.

This is the part where I come in ... as a former government official, I have lots of access to lots of different things ... particularly the media and lists of charitable individuals and organizations. You guys establish the front ... I spread the word, and I target the e-mails to the people who will actually give money to "the cause," unlike the barely successful scattershot approach that you currently employ.

I want 25% of said money for my services. I don't care what you guys do with your share. I guarantee you that we can raise a billion dollars in the next five years. If you believe me, reply to this, and welcome aboard. If you don't, it's your loss. Also, if you choose to not take part in this and so much as breathe a word to another living soul, your aforementioned status of flying below the radar will be raised to a massive public spectacle that'll make New York City's Mermaid Parade look like a funeral procession of the utmost gravity and decorum.

Also ... I'd like to note here that I am a FORMER Secret Service agent. I assure you that this is not a sting operation. Even if it were, this would clearly be entrapment and would be tossed out of court faster than you could say "mistrial."

So who's in?

Jonathan Land

Author's Note: I can't believe someone actually responded to this one.

SUBJECT: Re: A Fantastic Proposal Reply
TO: HASSAN MUSA
FROM: Jonathan Land <jland@incomplete.net>
DATE: 08/10/2002

DEAR JONATHAN LAND,

I HOPE THIS AMIL REACHES YOU IN GOOD HEALTH.I AM SORRY FOR REACHING YOU LATE. I HAVE BEEN ON RECESS LEAVE DUE TO MY HEALTH CONDITION.IF YOUR OFFER STILL STANDS I AM IN.COZ I AM IN SEARCH OF THE GREENER PASTURES IF YOU CAN PROVIDE ONE,THEN I AM ALL YOURS.

REGARDS,

HASSAN MUSA.

Dear Mr. Musa,

I'm so sorry to hear about your illness. When you say that you're looking for greener pastures, I can't tell if you want to be put out to them or not. What ails/ailed you, and are you doing better now? It doesn't sound like it. Please let me know, because I hate to see another human suffer. If you are still in pain, my amicable friend, I can help.

Now, assisted suicide is not legal here in America, but I can easily find out what the laws are in your jurisdiction. As I mentioned in my previous e-mail, I'm a former Secret Service agent, but I do have some medical training. I once performed a tracheotomy with a ballpoint pen on a baby I delivered in the backseat of a taxi stuck in an elevator that fell into a well. If it weren't for the unborn child's pet dog Lassie being able to so eloquently describe and then lead us to the location of the future Timmy, that well would be a festering pit of death that the authorities (such as myself) would discover only after the neighbors reported the stench.

That's no way to go, and whether you're stuck in an abandoned well, or dying of a terminal illness, it's a slow death, and no one wants that. Not you, not your family or beneficiaries, and certainly not the funeral home, which wants nothing more than to mark you off their schedule. I took the liberty of reading Dr. Jack Kevorkian's private FBI file to see how he does it (I have access to these things, you know). Frankly, it all seemed a little over my head with certain mixtures of chemicals being released at certain times, so I don't think that would be the ideal method if I were to assist you.

Then I got to thinking . . . what's with this sissy injection stuff? I've got access to government armories full of deadly weapons! Of course, I'm very good with a gun (which I never returned when my resignation was asked for), but just to play safe, I'm thinking: bazooka, 20 feet from your head. It'll be quick and easy, and your nerve endings will be atomized before the pain could hit them. (By the way, I hope you were thinking that your funeral would be a closed-casket deal. If not, I know one of those CIA makeup artists who does amazingly realistic work. We can throw a mask we'll make of your face on some other guy.)

So just say the word, and I'll see to it that that's the last word you say.

Now, just on the off chance that I misinterpreted what you wrote, and that you're fit as a fiddle, my scam offer still stands, but logistically I haven't received enough takers to be able to pull this off.

If you are not, in fact, dying, do you have any friends or associates that you feel are trustworthy enough to be a part of this? Remember, they MUST have clean records, and I will check any names you bring forth using the same methods that I used to check you out. I have far more to lose here than you do.

So how may I be of assistance?

Jonathan Land

jland@incomplete.net

Author's Note: Original spam donated by James T. Burr.

. . . .

SUBJECT: Re: RESPOND
TO: willam stewart
FROM: Jonathan Land <jland@incomplete.net>
DATE: 10/18/2002

IS A PLESURE WRITING YOU THIS E-MAILI AM WILLAM STEWART (ATTORNEY) MY CLI-
ENT MRS ESTRADA HAVE TOLD ME ABOUT A BUSINESS PROPOSAR TO YOU MR Jim Burr ALL
LEGAL PROCEEDURE HAVE BEEN CARRY OUT IN MY CHAMBER FOR FORMAL INTRODUCTION I
WILL LIKE YOU TO STATE TO ME HOW YOU ARE WELL, MADAM HAVE INSTRUCTED ME TO
GIVE YOU THE DETAILS OF THE PROPOSAR ONCE MORE WHICH SHE HAS EARLIER SEND TO
YOU BEFORE

Dear Jim burr

Listen and read carefully, I found your contact from the world trade center
and that is why I have decided to involve you in this transaction o.k, I am
a woman of substance and of great importance to my nation and the society
in general. I will not entertain any act of unserious ness from you in this
transaction o.k.

You must take instructions from me at all time and for security reasons you
will only communicate me only by my e-mail for now o.k. The business is This!!
!!!

I, am Mrs Louisa Ejercitor Estrada, the wife of Mr Joseph Estrada the former
president of Philippine located in the south East Asia. My husband was presently impeached from office by a backed uprising of mass demonstrators and
senate. During my husband's regime as president of Philippine, I realized US$
120.5 millions of dollars from various contract projects! I executed successfully. I had planed to invest this money in real estate and industrial
production.

Now I have used diplomatic means in moving this money to a security company in
(canada)as valuables, they do not know the contents of the boxes o.k. except
you and I

Now if you agree to carry out this business, I will give to you the information of the security company and you will be there to clear the boxes o.k.
There is no risk involved o.k, you will see the money for your self before any
thing, then you will open an account there and pay in the money after you have
cleared.

My husband is facing trails here with the Philippine government so my family's
life style is restricted and all my phone and other contracts are monitored by
the Philippine authority. I will offer you 25% of the total fund if you safely
clear this money from the security company, you must keep this business secret
AND confidential, not even your partner must know about this o.k until you are
through with this business. Once again, I want you to be honest, and faithful,
I shall delegate my Attorney to meet with you in (canada) on your arrival o.k.

So you must confirm your ticket to abroad immediately, and wait for my attorney's contact o.k, so confirm your ticket and after which I will give to you
the contacts of the security company in abroad o.k.

I hope we will build a solid business relationship, waiting to read from you
shortly o.k. Regards, and god bless us best regards

mrs estrada

PLEASE GO THROUGH AND MAIL TO ME WERE YOU ARE NOT CLEAR I EXPECT YOUR QUICK REPLY

BEST REGARD

WILLAM STEWAR

Mr. Stewart,

I have received your letter, which did help to clarify matters somewhat, regarding the proposal to aid Mrs. Estrada, wife of the former president of the Philippines, with security-sensitive financial transactions. I will be away attending to family matters for ten days and will not be using the Internet during that time. I suggest that between now and then you contact my business associate Jonathan Land, whom I believe will play a crucial role in the business deal you propose. He can be reached at jland@incomplete.net.

Sincerely,

James T. Burr

DEAR JONATHAN LAND

IS A PLESURE WRITTING YOU THIS E-MAIL, I WAS DIRECTED BY JAMES T.BURR TO CONTACT YOU ON A BUSINESS PPROPOSAL I SENT TO HIM TO CONTINUE DISCAUSION WITH YOU, HE TOLD ME THAT YOU ARE HIS BUSINESS ASSOCIATE AND THAT YOU ARE CAPABLE OF HANDLING THE BUSINESS TILL HE RETURN FROM HIS TEN DAYS JORNEY, I HOPE THAT HE HAS BRIF YOU VERY WELL ON THE BUSINESS IF SO WRITE ME IMMEDAITELLY AND THIS SAME TIME SEND ME YOUR COMPLETE DETAILS SO THAT I CAN CONTACT YOU IMMEDAITELLY. I EXPECT YOUR QUICK RESPOND. BEST REGARD

MR WILLAM STEWART

N/B

I AM AM ATTORNEY TO MRS ESTRADA THE WIFE OF THE FORMAL PRESIDENT OF PHILIPPINE.

Hello!

Sorry for my delay in responding. I was quite busy out on a mission pitting two factions of ne'er-do-wells against each other to mutually destruct each other so the rest of the peaceful villagers would no longer live in fear of violence or extortion.

As Mr. Burr mentioned, I am his business associate. I am a Canadian samurai under his employ. After being a masterless ronin for so long, it pleased me greatly that Mr. Burr saw that I would be of use to him after hacking several of his competitors' arms off. He brought me into his office, fed me rice and Moosehead beer (aka Canadian sake), and we got along famously. He is my amicable friend, as I wish you to be.

From what he tells me, you are wishing to transport money located in Canada to a bank in the United States for financial reasons I don't understand, beyond the fact that I'll be getting a cut of Mr. Burr's share.

I will need to know where this money is, how many men guard it, and if there are any known booby traps I should be aware of. Then I will assess the situation, gather enough men to do the job right (I usually work with seven), and then proceed with the operation.

Those donut-gulping, bad coffee-chugging rent-a-Mounties won't know what hit them, unless they perish slowly. Then they'll probably figure out that it was the searing blades of what will feel like a 120.5 million swords, a lash for every American dollar of yours they have in their possession.

Then we will transport the money safely and securely by rickshaw through an unprotected segment of the border into the U.S., and right up to the teller of Mr. Burr's bank. If the segment happens to be protected, we will unprotect it by striking down any Mountie in our path with the searing blades of 189.1 million swords, one for each Canadian dollar that we will be held responsible for (give or take, depending on the currency exchange rate on the day of the mission).

So give me the information I require, and I will immediately get to work.

Jonathan Land

Canadian Samurai and Business Associate to James T. Burr

CHAPTER 9

Sex Sells?

Do you have an unusual fetish? Probably not. If you do, it's very fortunate that your in-box has every creepy desire (as well as the standard ones) covered.

Here's just a small sampling of these e-mails and the reactions of whoever I'm claiming to be.

SUBJECT: Re: Young College Chicks!
TO: cupracefan
FROM: Jonathan Land <jland@incomplete.net>
DATE: 02/20/2001

Hi, my name is Amy. I'm a freshman at UCLA.

My sorority girlfriends and I just designed a website to help pay for college. We have hardcore pictures of us and our boyfriends having kinky sex. New pix are uploaded every day. Click Here To Enter

> Hi Amy!
>
> I'm so glad you wrote to me! My name is Jon, I'm a senior in high school, and I'm applying to UCLA! Do you have any words of advice? I know it's really hard to get in there, but my grades are good, and I got 1500 on my SATs (yay!). My interview's coming up next week! Also, are there any work-study jobs besides the e-commerce positions you referred to in your prospective student introductory letter, or is that not part of the financial aid package? I'm not good with computers. I couldn't even make your link work.
>
> Please help me! I don't know anyone else who goes there. I want to go to UCLA soooooooooooo bad!
>
> C Ya in September (I hope -- fingers crossed),
>
> Jon

SUBJECT: Re: VIDEOS OF BRITNEY SPEERS THAT YOU MUST SEE !'
TO: louise69x_.fem_bi
FROM: Jonathan Land <jland@incomplete.net>
DATE: 07/16/2001

THE ARE THE VIDEOS THAT BRITNEY SPEERS WANTS BANNED .. & WE HAVE THE VIDEOTAPE AND HEAPS MORE !!!! .

ITS ALL TOTALLY TASTY AND COOL !!!

CLICK HERE!

Britney Caught Sucking Cock!

http://[URL deleted]

My name is Jonathan Land, and I'm a volunteer for PETA, People for the
Ethical Treatment of Animals, and I actually took part in the incident referred
to above. Seeing as we're a nonprofit organization, I was hoping that we
could get some sort of deal on these tapes. We plan to distribute hundreds
of them to prominent media outlets. People need to see this for themselves.
I was actually protesting in the place where the event went down, but I didn't
have the foresight to bring a video camera.

I remember it so clearly though . . .

BEGIN FLASHBACK SEQUENCE

Britney Spears was touring down in Bogota, Colombia, and as part of her
record company duties, she had to be part of things like radio promos,
meet-and-greets, and on that day, she was the celebrity referee at a Pepsi-
sponsored cockfight. The match was about to begin. The announcer spoke
(this is a literal translation from the best of my recollection): "Welcome to
the PepsiDome. You can buy a grand assortment of Pepsi products from our
concession stands just outside the arena . . ." He takes a deep breath and
composes himself. "I am the most of please to introduce . . . Your reference
guest . . . Shakey Spears!"

If Britney hadn't been doing some lines from the mayor's private stash in the
little girls' room at the time of the announcement, she would have been livid
to hear her name butchered like that. She came out in time for the crowd to
give a giant "oooohhhh" and the minor applause that William Shakespeare
would warrant in this day and age.

My crude translation of the announcer continues: "And corner of left . . .
vroom vroom, always from Ireland, and is boy wings tired . . . Cockles . . .
O' . . . Ma . . . heart."

The audience booed.

"And right angle . . . is five-time champion . . . from Bogota . . . Cluck . . .
You . . . Up . . . GOOOOOOAAAAALLL . . . GOOOOOAAAAAAALLLL . . .
GOOOOOAAAAAAALLLLLLLLL!!!"

The audience ROARED.

Cluck You Up was obviously a local hero with roots in the community. He was
respected, yet feared. I could see his tattoos marking previous victories, and
whatever "Thug Life" translates to was written in Spanish across his stomach.
His grizzled, pock-marked beak led me to believe he was one hard pecker.

But that's not all I saw. As the standing ovation for Cluck You Up continued into its eighth minute, Britney seemed to be sobering up a little, and it dawned on her that she was being upstaged by a chicken. I caught a glimpse of her eyes as she started to panic. They were darting around the arena at all of Cluck You Up's rabid fans, and she did some sort of Julia Roberts impression:

"No, no . . . I'm the champion. Meee meeee . . . meeeeeeeeeeeeeeeeeee."

She then totally flipped. In a move that would make Ozzy Osbourne soil himself for salmonella reasons alone, she grabbed Cockles O' Maheart, bit his head off, and then threw him down and did a little touchdown victory dance. She then picked up Cluck You Up, bit HIS head off, spit it out, and then sucked all the blood out of his body, leaving him thin, limp, and wrinkly, like a rubber chicken with a skin graft from a feathered 90-year-old man. On his fourth lap around her legs, she picked up Cockles O' Maheart and did the same to him.

The vision of Britney Spears, a headless rooster in each of her hands, with blood dripping out of her mouth and collecting into a pool in her tightly bound cleavage is one I will NEVER forget.

Then she proceeded to sing.

It was truly horrible.

As if that weren't enough, violence erupted because the bookies were freaking out. Spears wasn't even on the card, and evidently this match would have had a huge payout. She made her escape in all of the confusion.

The news down there ran an article recently about how farmers have moved their chicken coops into their bedrooms at night because they fear the attack of the "Shrill Red-breasted Shrew." Some don't believe that that precaution is good enough.

END FLASHBACK SEQUENCE

We need to get the word out on this. Britney Spears must be stopped for her criminal abuse of animals. We need as many of those videotapes as you can provide us with at a nonprofit/educational rate, and frankly, my stick figure drawing of the events have not been convincing people about how real this whole thing is.

Can you please help us?

Jonathan Land, PETA

SUBJECT: Re: SCARE PEOPLE WITH YOUR HUGE COCK!
TO: exkhbasfja31890
FROM: Jonathan Land <jland@incomplete.net>
DATE: 10/02/2001

Subject: SCARE PEOPLE WITH YOUR HUGE COCK!

THINK YOU'RE BIG ENOUGH FOR HER?

LET US HELP YOU GET A BIGGER PENIS!

CLICK HERE TO ADD INCHES TO YOUR PENIS IN JUST DAYS... GUARANTEED

Dear Ma'am,

I'm not sure if I got the gist of your advertisement because I only speak Spanish, and I ran this through one of those Internet translators, but I do believe that this is my dream come true! You are a lifesaver. I am also using the same translator to write this back to you, so if my words seem less than eloquent and my sentences get mangled, you'll know why. That being said, here we go, and I hope this comes out right:

I need to get my hands on a scary, huge cock in the worst way possible. I'm the fight arranger for the PepsiDome in Bogota, Colombia. A few months ago we had a horrible tragedy involving guest referee Britney Spears and two of our champions. I won't get into the gory details, but we lost two of our prize performers, Cluck You Up, and Irish import Cockles O' Maheart, who are now both pecking corn in the Big Coop in the Sky.

We haven't had any more matches since that tragic bout. You must be thinking that in a venue such as the PepsiDome we must have a huge amount of casualties all the time. Such is not the case. We're very ethical here. Our cockfights are all well choreographed, like professional wrestling. All of our performers are well-trained ex-circus roosters. Some have reported to work after the Spears incident, but most of our finest cocks have been too afraid to come.

A kid at a local college edited together a version of "Chicken Run" with "Gladiator" that's been keeping everyone entertained, but we need to get back to live matches. I've been promoting a bout called Peck 'er Eyesout vs. Foghorn Killhorn, but Peck 'er Eyesout ducked out because he's a big sissy, and I need to replace him fast. I need a cock of immense proportions for the role, and at the moment I personally don't have anything that measures up. He also better be ready for action, because the fight is soon.

Let's do it. I'd like photos and prices of the best ASAP, and then I will give you my business.

Jonathan Land

Cock Handler

PepsiDome

✉

SUBJECT: Re: DO YOU LIKE HARDCORE PORN?
TO: acirillo
FROM: Jonathan Land <jland@incomplete.net>
DATE: 04/20/2001

DO YOU LIKE HARDCORE PORN?

IF YOUR ANSWER IS YES CLICK HERE TO SATISFY YOUR URGE!!

Dear You,

I never write letters like this, but since there is no option stated for a "no" response to your question, in your case, I'll make an exception.

No. I most certainly do not like hard-core porn. However, I simply adore soft-core pornography. Really soft-core. Like old married couples holding hands and gazing lovingly into each other's eyes with the quiet intensity that shows a true bond that can weather time and adversity. Oh my god, I am hard as a fucking rock now!

Do you have any porn sites handy where I can find pictures of that sort of thing? Like a woman in 1920s garb with a dainty yellow parasol sitting on a park bench while coyly observing a man wearing suspenders and a light, summery pair of dress pants? . . . uhhhhh-hhhuuhhhhu . . . Wow, I just soiled myself.

Where could I ever find anything like that???

Jon

⊠

SUBJECT: Re: startfreesex open !
TO: Karel
FROM: Jonathan Land <jland@incomplete.net>
DATE: 07/09/2001

Dear TGP-Master,

http://[URL deleted] opened its doors today, we would like to give you the opportunity to post some of your galleries on our site. Of course there is no obligation to put our banner on your Website, but it is always greatly appreciated.

Putting a lot of money and effort in the promotion of the project, we are confident on the result and success.

So why not give it a try and post your galleries today. Or even better, you can post galleries on every range of categories. We are NOT accepting Popups, Child porn and Bestiality. (We are very strict on these issues)

http://[URL deleted] is a database driven website. The galleries with the highest hit-rate will bed on top of the list. Better your galleries look, more hits you will get!

We hope to start a long-lasting (free) business relationship with you.

Kind regards,

Karel

I have some stuff I'd like to submit to your site. Two questions though:

1. Anything in particular that you're currently looking for?

2. How weird can the weird stuff get, short of the no-nos mentioned above?

Jon

SUBJECT: Re: Re: startfreesex open !
TO: Karel
FROM: Jonathan Land <jland@incomplete.net>
DATE: 07/09/2001

hi Jon,

we like amateur content very much.

soon we will open http://[URL deleted]

and also http://[URL deleted]

and also http://[URL deleted]

send us your weird stuff, either we place it now or you we can place it later.
please keep in touch,

regards,

karel

Great!

Well, I believe that the most erotic sexual organ is the mind, and I use pho-
tography to create what I like to consider to be challenging sexual images.
You mentally have to work for it, but it's worth it, and it'll get you off in the
end. Please note, the focal point of the last sentence was "get you off," not "in
the end." I'm not THAT kind of photographer.

Enclosed are 3 pictures from my collection. Give me the go-ahead, and I can
"hook you up" with many more.

They're entitled "Nude Descending a Staircase," "Japanese Schoolgirl," and
"All-Out Orgy," respectively. "All-Out Orgy" has a uncensored, European
version of "Eyes Wide Shut" thing going on that makes it a crowd pleaser.

Also, would it be possible to get a credit next to my images?

Thank you,

Jon

"Nude Descending a Staircase":

"Japanese Schoolgirl":

"All-Out Orgy":

SUBJECT: Re: Someone is interested in you
TO: Qi4yMzMuNjM5NTc0OA
FROM: Jonathan Land <jland@incomplete.net>
DATE: 07/31/2002

Hello.

I'm not particularly graceful socially (physically either, but I realize that you can't assist me in that respect), so I thought I'd run this by you to see if you think it'll be appropriate for your service, and if you believe it'll help me in the quest for The One. Here it goes:

Twenty-something skeptic looking for someone to love me as much as I hate myself.

I'm a lot of work, but I know women like a project with potential! I can safely say I have potential, because I'm so miserable, low, and unaccomplished that beyond a shadow of a doubt, the only way I could fall farther is if I started flinging my poop at others or lighting it on fire as a member of the Al Queda network. I could rid the world of myself, but no one would know I'd be gone. I fly so low under the radar that I crawl . . . usually drunk in sleazy biker bars.

Your constant reassurance will be essential for me to stave off my dark demons of depression. Don't feel bad if I hurt myself. It won't be the first time, and it certainly won't be the last. It doesn't mean you're a lousy girl-friend. It just means that you're not the right one to keep my fragile psyche in check. No pressure, and in advance, I'd like to say that it's not your fault.

I require lots of alone time, which will benefit you the more you realize that I'm intolerable. I like going places and doing things, even if all the places and things are under my roof. And don't try to get me to go on vacation. It's a silly idea anyway, since I don't work to begin with. My life's like one big party where I sit by the door hoping for no one to arrive. If you try to get me to dance or talk to me about God, I will completely flip out on you.

I like to go Dutch both in restaurants (whenever you can get me to go to one) and in bed where we'll each be responsible for taking care of our own parts. My monetary and sexual selfishness is something I'm working on. Recently I've begun paying for sex, so that's a bold step in dealing with the former, and it opens the window of opportunity for dealing with the latter. I'm no good at picking up women, and treating them well if I'm able to find a sucker. A lot of people who used to be friends with me say that I objectify women, but it's not true. I only objectify the good parts.

I'd prefer someone young and naive who I can mold into my image or break trying. Emotional baggage is a big no-no. If you've had any serious past loves, I can't compete with that, nor do I want to hear about it. The right woman for me is one who doesn't know any better than to be with me. I'd prefer to be with an impressionable young girl who I could be condescend-ing to, and who thinks that "condescending" is either the process of moisture forming in the cold or a convict falling farther from grace.

Okay, here's my good quality:

I can make you laugh real hard. Where lots of guys have a good sense of humor that'll make you laugh till you cry. I'll prefer to make you cry till you laugh. I think I can bludgeon you with so much of my own misery that you'll be able to eventually break into hysterics as your frayed and tattered nerves are completely exposed and you no longer know how to react to any facet of your daily life.

I know this description makes me out to seem fairly undesirable, but I guarantee that everyone else here is exactly like me . . . they just aren't as forthcoming and explicit about it as I am. So even though I'm being perfectly reasonable, I'm sure I'll be looked over, and shame on you for doing so! As a matter of fact, if you don't reply to this desperate cry for help, you are a truly wretched human being. So there! The irony is that if I were some sullen goth chick on here, everyone would find this all adorable, and my in-box would be flooded with suitors. Thanks bartender -- make that a double!

You know what, don't even reply to this. You make me ill. Just leave me the hell alone. I can't deal with your shit, keep me out of it.

Jonathan Land

✉

SUBJECT: Re: meet me in the same place LKCKBU
TO: jody2
FROM: Jonathan Land <jland@incomplete.net>
DATE: 01/02/2002

Hi There! My name is Kathy, I'm trying to put my self though school so my girlfriends and I decided to put up a web site featuring my friends and I doing all sorts of nasty little things with each other and the campus guys! My favorite past time is giving head and you can see me right on the front page of the site BTW I'm the blonde in the bottom right hand corner. Click in and see me now!

Listen. Kid. You're going about this all wrong. There are hundreds of millions of porn sites out there, and here you are, thinking: Look at meeeeee, I'm naaaaaaked and I have a gimmiiiiiiick: I'm a naaaaked schooooooolgirrrrrrl. Oooh, I haven't seen THAT one before. That's as original as (insert race here) porn.

I'm sorry to break this to you, Hon, but the naughty schoolgirl thing with the plaid skirt getup, glasses, and suggestively placed apple near your privates just doesn't cut it anymore. Now, if you could core the apple with your privates, THAT would be something. Unfortunately, it would probably leave most male viewers perplexed and in fear for their own genitalia. Still, I and a countless number of Japanese businessmen would pay top dollar to see that.

These days you need a REAL gimmick . . . and I've got one for you. First of all, let me introduce myself: I am World Class Pornographer, Jonathan Land.

You're probably too young to recall my most famous work. It was in the 80s when I discovered "Russian" porn stars Yerkov Komzalot and Zbigone Putinmi and was able to capitalize on the end-of-the-Cold-War successes of performers such as that ballet guy, Yakov Smirnof, and . . . uhhh . . .

OH! I'll also have you know that my best-known film from that period, "White Russian/Black Russian," predated the suspiciously similar "Jungle Fever" by 10 years, and what my movie lacked in sets, costumes, plot, dialog, and acting, it made up for in not having Spike Lee involved. It was a fascinating exploration into how Russians of different ethnicities still had the common river of vodka flowing through them. Plus, it had a money shot that made the Macy's 4th of July celebration in New York look as spectacular as a snuffed-out birthday candle. It was Oscar caliber, but it's very difficult to get porn nominated. However, it was awarded with a Woody by anyone who's ever seen it. My only regret about the movie is the joke about the "horrible Fyodor" in the oral sex scene, which would have been good if I were still using laugh tracks like I was in the 70s, but no one wants to hear laughter while they're getting naked, except for dirty movie star Molesto the Clown.

I digress. I want to help you because you seem ambitious. Plus, you're obviously poor, you want to make money, and since you're young and impressionable, you'll probably do anything.

I went to your enclosed link, but it was broken like most of the legitimate dreams of girls I knew who I personally turned to a life of trivialized, graphic sex for the entertainment of others. I wish inner beauty counted here, but it doesn't. If you look like you were beaten by the ugly stick (the figurative one, not French porn star Francois Ugly's "love bayonet"), I can't help you.

My gimmick is as follows: I'm starting a self-help pornography television series called "Chicken Soup for Your Hole." It will be a fascinating exami- nation of how women can enrich their lives through sex. This is where you come in: you would be the host of the show, and you would show the women how to gain more confidence, find inner peace, and acquire greater self- awareness by having sex with an obscene number of men in ridiculously absurd ways. An edited version will appear on the Oxygen network. The tagline is "Chicken Soup for Your Hole -- It's Hole-istic." Good, huh?

So that's it. Basically, if I can determine from your picture that you don't look like you were hit by multiple trucks, you've got the job. Unless, of course, your schoolgirl gig is raking in the big bucks. If you want to do business, show me what you've got, and let's make some television magic.

Jonathan Land

World Class Pornographer

SUBJECT: Re: Incest Porn! 28043
TO: d21488
FROM: Jonathan Land <jland@incomplete.net>
DATE: 01/02/2002

Close relatives.

Evidence records from Max Hashly secret diary.

Family inside. Grandparents give grandkids sex lessons.

Dad & Daughter. Young girl cannot control her urges.

Sister & Brother. Sister uses game to teach brother about masturbation.

Family party. Hide & seek becomes an exciting experience.

Click on the link to access Incest porno instantly.

CLICK HERE

Important! Please notice, the specific of this web site is that all individuals filmed or depicted are not younger than 18 years of age. Due to this fact
CLOSE RELATIVES stands out from other sites of similar content.

Excellent. Thy solicitation pleaseth me greatly.

My name is Jonathan Land, Prince of Caspiar, a small island country in the
Caspian Sea. My 15th birthday draws near, and it is time for me to take a
wife. For centuries we have been able to sustain our lineage solely upon
the Royal Family of Caspiar, but a mystery epidemic has fallen upon us and
grows stronger with each generation. Our women can no longer breed, and
our wounds do not heal.

I have an amusing anecdote about the latter that I will casually relate to thee
now. I was once having the most splendid vigorous intercourse with my sister. After we had completed the act, I noticed blood of the future queen on
the bed, emanating from her unmentionables. I said, "Princess, thou art far
too thin and far too young to conceive, why art thou bleeding?" With her last
bit of energy, she shrugged. Oh, we laughed as I watched the flow of blood
slow to a halt through her translucent skin.

Those were the days. As much as it doth pain me, my family, and the citizens
of our great nation, I must take a fantastic journey to find a bride elsewhere.
She must be of a royal bloodline, and thick-skinned, both physically for our
family's preservation, and emotionally for the occasional ribbing and josh-
ing that doth occur at our lavish banquets. From thy brief communication,

I can tell that the Hashlys that thou referrest to art of good stock, but I need to know more before I engage both the girl and my fleet to sail to her.

Where do they come from? How far back doth their family go, and how pure is their bloodline? Also, if thou couldst ballparketh the dowry, I would be much obliged. I will need to know these things before I can make an appropriate proposal to the youngest of the Hashly girls.

Jonathan Land, Prince of Caspiar

P.S. I trust thou wilt respond to me promptly, since we are doing this on the computer. Thou dost know, computers saved the people of Caspiar. Parchment cuts were the leading cause of death in Caspiar previously. It helped us stockpile our country's leading export, type AB negative blood, but many lives were sacrificed for our economic stability. Hail Caspiar!

Author's Note: Original spam donated by Natalie Diffloth.

SUBJECT: Re: Watch Teen Farm Girls Have Sex with their animals Free! ltilwvaw
TO: farmnlmwqxry
FROM: Jonathan Land <jland@incomplete.net>
DATE: 09/25/2002

SEE Teen Farm Girls Have Sex with their animals Free! You think you have seen some pretty crazy porn on the internet? YOU HAVEN'T SEEN SHIT! I saw the most unbelievable movie clip ever to grace the internet! These guys put up a clip of a beautiful teen farm girl who actually fucks her horse!NO BULLSHIT,SHE ACTUALLY FUCKS A HORSE WITH A 31 INCH COCK!

THE MOVIE QUALITY IS GREAT AND HAS SOUND TOO! IT IS UNBELIEVABLE! THIS LITTLE SLUT CAN REALLY HANDLE A GIANT HORSE COCK IN HER TIGHT LITTLE TEEN PUSSY LIKE YOU WOULD NOT BELIEVE! YOU HAV TO WATCH THIS CLIP BEFORE SOMEONE FINDS IT AND TAKE IT OFF.

HERES THE GOOD PART. THESE GUYS AREN'T A NORMAL PORN SITE SO THEY DON'T WANT MONEY TO LET US WATCH SO ITS FREE. BUT WHAT THEY DO IS MAKE YOU TAKE THIS TEST THAT ASKS HOW BIG A HORSE DICK IS. THAT'S SOMETHING THAT ONLY PEOPLE INTO ANIMAL SEX WOULD KNOW. SO I THINK THEY ARE JUST TRYING TO MAKE SURE YOU ARE SOMEONE WHOS INTO THIS STUFF..NOT SOMEONE WHO WANTS TO BUST THEM. SO IF YOU'RE LIKE ME AND DON'T KNOW ANYTHING ABOUT ANIMALS JUST GUESS THE SIZE. THERE ARE ONLY 3 CHOICES AND IF YOU GET IT RIGHT YOU'RE IN. YOU GET TO WATCH THE WHOLE

CLIP..AND HEY DO NOT FORGET TO SAVE IT CUZ YOU'LL WANT TO WATCH IT AGAIN OR SHOW IT TO YOUR FRIENDS LATER!CLICK ON THE LINK BELOW TO WATCH THIS LITTLE SLUT FUCK HER HORSE FOR 8 MINUTES! DO NOT FORGET TO SAVE IT SO YOU CAN WATCH IT AGAIN LATER!

Hello.

My name is Jonathan Land, and I'm an Animal Psychologist with the ASPCA.

I've always thought that bestiality was a myth . . . a story that farmers tell their children to show them the difference between right and wrong, should they ever think that their livestock want to be more than just friends or food. This shocking reality is a wake-up call that's more maddening than a thousand dogs humping any given leg simultaneously.

Just because horses happen to be hung like themselves doesn't mean that they should be the object of sexual abuse, nor that they should procreate with humans, forging a race of centaurs that will be both subject to the scorn of the human world and the base confusion of the animal one. While every track and field coach in the world would benefit from such creatures being on the team, and racing jockeys would all be put out of work, this is not the way of nature!

Just because bunnies like to "do it" like they do, that doesn't mean that they're voracious nymphomaniacs for any lonely guy who has no luck with a human woman. No, they're the prey for other animals in that kingdom, not ours. And when a cat's in heat, they're not giving you "the look." They want one of their own, and we can all blame those hot actresses who've played Catwoman over the years for propagating that fallacy.

I've enclosed a simple pamphlet about the proper way to mount a horse. I've never had to distribute it before, but now I'm glad that we had these printed up.

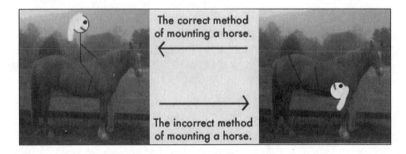

The correct method of mounting a horse.

The incorrect method of mounting a horse.

Please stop this now, or my organization will take action.

Jonathan Land

Animal Psychologist

American Society for the Prevention of Cruelty to Animals (ASPCA)

CHAPTER 10
Spam Potpourri: Part 2

--- ✉ ---

Here's more shouting into the abyss for you. The spammers these were sent to
will never know what they've missed, nor will they care.

--- ✉ ---

SUBJECT: Re: Upgrade to first class
TO: gposb
FROM: Jonathan Land <jland@incomplete.net>
DATE: 09/07/2001

Twelve-year old Travel Agency seeks Independent Travel Agents!

All Agents receive their I.A.T.A. Photo ID Card along with a personalized website which contains an online TravelDesk for booking airfares, hotels, and much more!!

YOU WILL NOT FIND A BETTER DEAL THAN THIS ANYWHERE ELSE IN AMERICA!!!20

LOW STARTUP!!!

For more information send an email to or click here

http://[URL deleted]

Hello,

My name is Jonathan Land, and I'm an Independent Travel Agent. I'm currently managing only one client, but this kid is a natural talent. I think with my business savvy and his skill, we can take the travel world by storm by providing a brand-new service that'll revolutionize scenic travel.

I discovered him on a Delta flight from Newark, NJ, down to Miami. I was going there to view "The Sweaty Palm," a tree that had a picture of a very nervous Mother Theresa on it, rendered in some form of mystery condensation that some poor sap was sending out press releases about. She was probably nervous because the tree was located outside of the sullied sex club, "The Hairy Palm," which wasn't her scene, either as a human or a possible projection. Anyhow, I needed to meet this guy to see if I wanted to run a story goofing on him for Comedy Central's "The Daily Show" with Jon Stewart, where I'm a segment producer (the travel agent thing is a part-time venture).

So here I was, about an hour early for my flight, sitting at the gate with about ten similarly time-anal passengers, when all of a sudden this guy wearing a green jumpsuit saying "Baggage Handler," a pilot's hat, and a little pin of wings pops up. He said, "Get in, we go, we go now, go go go, now now now, time is right!" and then made little airplane noises and performed a little simulation with his right hand of a plane taking off.

Three people went to the ticketing area to find out what the hell was happening, but the other seven of us got on because a flight's a flight, and the novelty of not leaving late made us all giddy.

I wish I was given more of a heads up so I had time for the valium to become effective, but I just hopped into the plane's restroom, broke the mirror, chopped the stuff up with one shard, and did a few lines off of a bigger chunk through a thinly rolled straw of that superhard airplane toilet paper. I'm the MacGuyver of tranquilizers! I sat down, buckled up, and hoped that no one would associate me with the bathroom damage.

Right from the start, this flight was a little different than the ones we're all accustomed to. Normally there's at least one flight attendant visible and some announcements before take-off concerning passenger safety and what to do in case of an accident, but the pilot was obviously having none of that.

And then we were off. I got my crossword book out, and I was trying to look for a puzzle that had no words like "explosion," "fire," or "Denver," but every one of them had the word "down," which was just SO ominous. So I put that away and played turtle by pulling my shirt over my head until we reached cruising altitude.

When I surfaced about an hour into the trip, I realized two things: (1) the turbulence was the worst I had ever experienced, like we were flying over potholes, and (2) we were flying startlingly low. My clue was when I saw the exit sign for Philadelphia on the New Jersey Turnpike roughly at eye level. At first I thought it was normal, because we were on one of those huge 777s that would naturally require a longer runway, but then my suspicions got the best of me.

I went up to the cockpit to find out what the deal was. When I slid the door back, I saw that the pilot was the same guy in the jumpsuit from before. "Gobackensitdonna," he said, as he shooed me away. I sat down in the co-pilot's seat to have a heart to heart.

"Hi, my name's Jon. What's yours?"

"Me pilot."

"OK, Pilot," I said. "I'm a little curious. Do you mind telling me why we're on the ground still?"

"Go Miami."

"Uhh . . . yeah, Go Miami!!! Rah rah rah, what's the spread?"

We were both totally confused now, and since my valium was in the middle of its peak effect, I was processing things very slowly. Half an hour later,

I looked through the window and I saw that we were coming up on the Delaware Memorial Bridge toll booth.

"Listen," I said, "We're coming to the last stop on the turnpike, and the toll on this thing's going to be killer. I think we should hop the turnstile on this one, especially since you didn't grab the ticket at the entry point!"

"Eh?"

"GO OVER!"

"Eh?"

"FLY!"

"Okee-dokee!"

He then fired up the jets, pulled back on the controls, and we hopped over the thing beautifully and landed with grace and poise. It's like we just floated over it. He seemed very surprised that he did it. I, however, had confidence in the little guy.

We came upon another toll plaza immediately afterward. He said, "Watch." He cracked open the left window and then jumped it like before, but this time . . . I swear to God . . . he dropped the 50-cent toll right in the little basket in midair . . . nothing but net. We slapped each other five and drove on.

At this point I was thinking what a shame it was that I wasted all of that valium on a clearly non-panic situation. This guy was good. I didn't know who he was, or why he had hijacked a plane to Miami, but his heart was in the right place. He wasn't malicious or dangerous, just a guy on a good old-fashioned joyride.

I realized I had been away from the main cabin for longer than I expected, and that I should probably make up something to tell the other passengers. I said that I was actually a Delta flight attendant and I explained to them that they were part of a pilot program (so to speak) that combined the fun of scenic travel with the speed of flight.

"Well, this doesn't seem to be particularly speedy," said one curmudgeonly old man.

I was prepared for this comment.

"We here at Delta appreciate your comments, and as a commitment to our stellar service, we will do everything possible to make your Delta experience the platonic ideal of scenic aviary travel. As a matter of fact, I'll go up to the pilot right now and see if we can remedy this situation."

I went to talk with the pilot. I noticed that the freeway traffic was awful, all backed up at the toll booth for the Harbor Tunnel in Baltimore. We couldn't hop over it, so he was going through it. By the time I questioned his decision, we were already in the tunnel shooting off bright yellow sparks as we scraped the sides. I figured out how to turn on the plane's Muzak system, and I blasted it.

I ran back to the cabin to see the effect. It was beautiful, and the little fireworks display appeased everyone.

"Is this great or what, people? Let's hear it for Delta!!! Come on, give it up!"

They all cheered. Now, more than ever, I realized I was a part of something special.

To cut a long story short, after we got out of the tunnel, I told my pilot friend to hit the gas on those open stretches of highway. We needed to deliver on my speedy promise, plus we had to lose those many police cars and helicopters on our tail. I left the Muzak up so the passengers wouldn't hear the sirens, but with the jets going, it was a moot point.

At one point I did ask the pilot, "Why go Miami?" He said the following:

"Before me no (makes hand motion of plane taking off), now me (makes hand motion of plane taking off)."

"So you've just always wanted to be a pilot, and now's your time to shine?"

"No, now me (makes hand motion of plane taking off)."

Then he took something out of his pocket to help explain his motivation. It was a vial of that "Natural Viagra" stuff that's advertised in people's e-mail all of the time. I don't know if I was more impressed that he responded and got the product, or that the product apparently worked.

"Now me (makes hand motion of plane taking off). Me babymaker now. Me go find sweetie."

I got a little more info when I pointed out that it was starting to storm, and he seemed a little scared. I said, "I'm no meteorologist, but I think we'll get through this okay."

To which he said, "You no meaty urologist! Meaty urologist say, 'no (makes hand motion of plane taking off) again.' Me now (makes hand motion of plane taking off). You believe. You help me babymaker with sweetie. You good guy!"

"I see . . . Well go Miami!"

"Go Miami!!!"

This man's intentions were good. He wasn't trying to simply bang the only two women on the plane, like I was. He was finding his sweetie and trying to start a family, and if this guy's progeny are even half as kind, intelligent, brave, and adept as he is, then the world will be that much better a place.

We made it to Miami in about 15 hours. I called up Pilot's estranged girl-friend to tell her the good news about Pilot's virility, and that she should meet him at a hotel, since her house would be swarming with cops. She was amazed at the measures he took to be with her once again as a "whole man." We jetted the last hour, and he and his sweetie had a very intense, passion-ate, and loving ten minutes together before the cops detained him.

I'm currently living with Pilot's pregnant girlfriend, awaiting his release from jail in another six months. I feel like I owe it to the guy to take care of her (for once I don't mean that sexually) in his absence, and provide for her and their daughter until he's able to.

Once he gets out, we plan on starting up our little travel venture together. Sightseeing by plane. We call it PilotLand Tours. Pilot and I are an excellent team. All we need is a plane, and we're good to go. We'd be a great asset to your travel company, and we'd greatly benefit from your financial support to get us off the ground . . . not that we'd get off of the ground, of course. :)

Thank you, and I hope to hear from you,

Jonathan Land,

CEO, PilotLand Tours, LLC

✉

SUBJECT: Re: Interested In Listing Jonathan Land In Our New Directory
TO: Jennifer Lochary
FROM: Jonathan Land <jland@incomplete.net>
DATE: 01/09/2002

Hello Jonathan,

My name is Jennifer Lochary and I work in Partnerships and Acquisitions here at Interservers.

We at Interservers are always attempting to find innovative ways to increase our market presence, and increase the value of our services to our customer base. Every so often, we have customers requesting services from us that we do not offer. These include services that Jonathan Land provides. About 6 months ago, we came up with the concept of assembling a "directory" of service pro-viders that performed services our customers sometimes ask for, and then have that list available to our customers for searching.

What we did was compile a list of companies in different areas that we thought might be appropriate, and now we are sending out an email to the database to get an initial read on whether this makes sense to the companies we have decided to approach.

We are interested in adding you to our list of companies that we have a preferred relationship with...and if it makes sense, possibly even partnering with Jonathan Land in some areas to reciprocate an offering of services. There are not costs or purchase requirments to participate.

This is a massive project for us Jonathan, and we are interested in finalizing our list of potential vendors/partners within the next few months. If you are interested and would like me to contact you to discuss this further, or if you would like more information, please respond to this email and let me know.

If you feel Jonathan Land would not be a fit and would not like us to consider you, there is no need to respond. If we do not hear back from you within a reasonable time we will assume you are not interested and remove you from our list.

I look forward to hearing from you.

Sincerely,

Jennifer Lochary

--->Accounts Starting as Low as $2.95 per month!<----

--->Professional Web Sites Starting as Low as $95 Dollars!<----

I would be quite honored to be included in your directory. I'd imagine that I would have my own section heading, because I provide quite a unique service.

My name as it should appear in print: Dr. Jonathan Land

My title as it should appear in print: Worthy Adversary

I am multitalented, thanks to my Ph.D. in liberal arts from Harvard, and fiercely competitive, due to my insatiable lust to garner the respect of all dignified people. I hire myself out to people who want a challenge, or who just need an enemy to keep them on edge.

Some of my critics call me an "intellectual whore," but that term is limited and demeaning. I will partake in any physical competition as well. I am not simply a brain in a jar. All I ask for is a reasonable amount of training time. Then I will accomplish any task set before me, or I will fail admirably and supply a full refund.

I will do anything, anytime, anywhere, better than anyone else. Whether it's a water-cooler argument with a coworker or an Olympic event, a battle of the bands or an eating contest, a science fair or a board game, I will emerge victorious and be held in the highest regard by my opponents.

But don't just take my word for it. Here are some quotes from people who've had the opportunity to have the taste of defeat served to them by my able hand:

"Jonathan Land consistently beats our lowest prices. Because of cutbacks, I didn't get my holiday bonus. That hurts, but I have no one to blame but myself for not having Land's bold marketing vision."

- Jim Franklin, Vice President of Sales, Circuit City, Inc.

"Dr. Land got my client 25-to-life . . . for indecent exposure! I'm keeping him on retainer as my lawyer."

- Johnny Cochran, Lawyer

"He slapped me sillier. I give him mad props. He's got game and a cute butt that's like two turtle shells oscillating in perfect rhythm when he walks."

- Mike Tyson, Heavyweight Boxer

"Jon Land rocks! R-O-C-K-S. Rocks."

- Frances Mueller, Runner-up, Li'l Tykes Day Care Center Spelling Bee, 1998

So there you have it. Put me on the list, and let's do business.

Dr. Jonathan Land

Worthy Adversary

✉

Author's Note: If you read this, I'll have to kill you.

SUBJECT: Subject: Re: Your Military Benefits are Waiting!
TO: MailCenter
FROM: Jonathan Land <jland@incomplete.net>
DATE: 07/08/2002

Dear Jonathan

Your military service has earned you valuable benefits that can save you money!

Use your GI Bill to earn your degree -- and a higher salary! Get free information from schools that value your military experience at Military.com.

Use your VA loan benefits to buy a home with no down payment or to refinance
your current mortgage at a lower interest rate! Check out your VA eligibility
-- see how much house you can afford and how much money you can save!

Thank you so much! Your offer actually made me cry. I can't tell you what a
pleasant surprise it was to receive this e-mail. Really . . . I can't . . . but I will.

I literally just got back from a covert mission that you might have heard
about involving the assassination of the Afghani vice president. We had our
doubts about where the guy's loyalties were, so I did what I was always told
to do in these situations: I made up his mind for him once and for all.

Being a secret agent for the U.S. Armed Forces is very rewarding, but I've
never felt like I was a member of the club. I train and work in seclusion. I
don't get a battalion to bunk with, a subscription to "Stars and Stripes," or
even an Officer's Club where I can play musical grabass around a dark,
smoky pool table with the low-ranking female officers. Ahhh, I guess they're
not my type anyway. I like the officers . . . but I LOVE the privates.

Don't get me wrong . . . I love my country . . . and picking off a new, or even
a well-established enemy of The State gives my heart a flutter like falling in
love for the first time again and again. I've gotten to travel to foreign lands,
submerge myself in different cultures, and learn a dictionary's worth of eth-
nic slurs against small countries that aren't even on most world maps.

Of course, now that I've told you this, you can look forward to spending the
next and final 10 seconds of your life looking over your shoulder, running
from your desk in a big office that's about to have a big "accident." Hey . . .
you smell gas?

Thank you, though. This has been something I've been meaning to get off
my chest for quite some time. I'll remember this at least as far as my trip to
Cuba to execute Operation Thorn Out Of Side.

Jonathan Land

Secret Agent

Covert Ops., U.S. Armed Forces

*Author's Note: Spam donated by Meryl Yourish at http://www.yourish.com.
However, if you go to the site, I will get upset.*

SUBJECT: Re: yourish.com
TO: cattledriver
FROM: Jonathan Land <jland@incomplete.net>
DATE: 01/16/2002

Hi my name is Dave I was surfing through the Internet and I saw you in Yahoo.

I hope I am emailing the right contact Meryl Yourish at yourish.com.

Anyway I am a Search Engine Guru and I have developed a strategy and unique technology to get in the top of any search engine. Since you are already doing some type of advertising in Yahoo , I know I can help you out and save you money.

In today's Internet Economy everything is about performance. I know I can help drive traffic to yourish.com and lots of it. I am so confident you will like my service, It's only $5 to sign up.

After the first month, it is only .25 a click with a small monthly fee. That's all there is to it. I hope that sounds good to you. I look forward to hearing some kind of response.

Please get back at your earliest convience - cattledriver or you can go here http://[URL deleted]

Since I saw you in Yahoo. I figured you could use my help.

Thanks

Dave

Dear Dave the CattleDriver,

I read my girlfriend's e-mail as I always do while she lies sound asleep in bed. As a responsible boyfriend, it's my duty to make sure that I can trust her as much as she claims I can. To date, she has proven to be completely trustworthy, except on one occasion. She told me that a particular Christmas gift was, and I quote, "not that expensive." I was able to determine by seeing her online receipt that it was, in fact, more than we agreed to spend on each other. I don't appreciate being lied to like that.

Fortunately, since I saw the e-mail about her order from Amazon.com before Christmas, I was able to adjust the gift I bought for her into the new, unspoken appropriate price range, and feigned a little extra surprise when the gift was properly revealed to me on Christmas day.

Meryl's an excellent girlfriend. A keeper, as they say. She's also a far better human being than I ever intend to be. However, I'm not entirely sure if she's aware of this, but she still appears to be smitten after three months of dating. She says so to her family on the phone. I have the wiretap recordings to prove it. I know I'm not the ideal mate for her, but as long as she remains oblivious to that important detail, I'm in the clear.

Since I intend to be with her as long as possible, it's my duty to ensure that she meets as few new people as possible. I also attempt to thin out her herd of friends by replying to their e-mail from her own account in the most insulting way possible. I've also constructed a library of recordings of her voice that I can play back with a touch of a button whenever she gets a call and I'm the only one in her house. These things have been working very well. Many a Friday night has been spent snuggling on the couch and watching movies, since my skilled manipulation has caused us to no longer be invited anywhere by anyone.

See where this is going? I saw your e-mail to Meryl from a few days ago, and it horrified me. Thanks to the damn Internet, she thinks it's her duty to put one of those weblogs up. It's easy to keep people away from her by driving them away psychologically and physically, but it's a lot harder to keep them away from a Web site.

Not only have you found her on Yahoo, but you want to further promote the site. Please, back off. She doesn't want your service. Never contact her again.

I'm working on developing the first cyber-restraining order that will require all visitors to yourish.com to keep at least 50 links away, and buddy, you're first on the list.

Jonathan Land

SUBJECT: Re: Aliens or Time Travelers PLEASE HELP!
TO: IneedTimeTravel
FROM: Jonathan Land <jland@incomplete.net>
DATE: 04/24/2002

If you are a time traveler or alien disguised as human and or have the technology to travel physically through time I need your help!

My life has been severely tampered with and cursed!!

I have suffered tremendously and am now dying! I need to be able to: Travel back in time.Rewind my life including my age back to 4. I am in very great danger and need this immediately!

I am aware of two types of time travel one in physical form and the other in energy form where a snapshot of your brain is taken using either the dimensional warp or the carbon copy replica device and then sends your consciousness back through time to part with your younger self. Please explain how safe and what your method involves.

I have a time machine now, but it has limited abilitys and is useless without a vortex.

If you can provide information on how to create vortex generator or where I can get some of the blue glowing moon crystals this would also be helpful. I am however concerned with the high level of radiation these crystals give off, if you could provide a shielding that would be great. I believe the vortex needs to be east-west polarized, North-south polarized vortexexs are used for cross-dimensional time travel only.

Only if you have this technology and can help me exactly as mentioned please send me a (SEPARATE) email to: IneedTimeTravel

Please do not reply if your an evil alien!

Thanks

Hello!

My name's Jonathan Land, and I am a doctor who has successfully negotiated the "physical form" of time travel you mention above. Please communicate to your brain that I am not an alien of the evil type. Really, I assure you I am not. Should your brain begin to feel comfortable and let its guard down, that is acceptable, for no harm shall come to you by my "hand." I am your amicable friend.

I'm sure you'd like to get the rolling balls, so I will inform you how to proceed in acquiring my assistance for your plight. Look at the following digital photograph. Study it. Not like a spawned progeny in one of your education factories studies manipulation of the numeric alphabet! Really study it. When you want to contact me, replicate the design in an open field. No one must see you. If they do, then they are an intoxicated farmer.

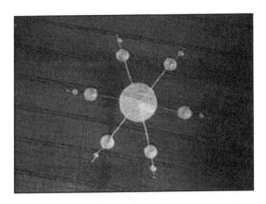

I will see this from high atop my vacation home at the "Red Planet Ranch."
I will then descend to the coordinates where the marking has been made
like the half-bat, half-man creature depicted in your illustrated serialized
folklore and increasingly intolerable motion pictures. Or you can e-mail me
here with your address. Either way, I hope your brain still believes that I am
not an evil alien. If not, your brain must be thinking that I am an illegal alien
in your United States country . . . yes . . . that works . . . I am from your Earth's
Mexico. Hola, my amicable amigo.

I will arrive (alone, not with 50 or so comrades) at the location of the inscrip-
tion in a large flying craft. This is merely a high-tech gadget with nothing
alien about it. I bridge the gap between my base income and my expenses
by being a spy. It is standard-issue spy transportation. Or I acquired it in a
casino battle from a pirate. It was like stealing candy from a baby, and then
eating both the candy and the baby. Whatever lulls your brain's suspicion
cortex and helps you sleep at night.

You will then be pulled aboard my vessel by a tractor beam. It is like an
Earth tractor, but it works vertically. We use it to till the Earth soil on our
Mexican walls. Just step into the light, and ride it up. NO MORE QUESTIONS!
You will not die at that particular point.

Now is when we begin to prepare you for time travel. I will outline the process so it will appear that my sole concern is your best interest, and that the
eating of your brain has not yet occurred to me as the prime motivation and
the inevitable conclusion of our encounter.

As I mentioned before, I am a doctor. I will remove your digestive tract
(that's the Earth Greek term for the medical test), then I will extract your
sperm with my strawlike pincers by puncturing your testicles as if they were

mini juice boxes. I will then take the sperm and grow new humans. Speaking of which, the one thing that I ask in return for my benevolent assistance is that you bring an Earth female of child-bearing age with you so I may implant the sperm into her for child making. Call it a date. Be sure to woo her with flowers and chocolate. The woman will be essential. Like your Bob Marley sang: "no woman, no time travel." See? I can relate to you, because I am not an evil alien! Are you no longer apprehensive?

Finally, I will eject a special type of corrosive bile on your head from my "mouth." This will easily remove your flesh and bone so I can delicately wriggle one or more of my "tongues" around the ridges of your brain. You might feel a tickling sensation, along with involuntary memory recall and bodily movement. It will not last long because I will remove your body promptly.

Then I will ship you piece by piece through the vortex, back in time so you will be four Earth years again. Please make sure you have someone on the other side because (a) they will need to reassemble you, and (b) I am returning you to an age where you will be an unaccompanied minor.

I hope to hear from you soon, and I love you for your mind!

Dr. Jonathan Land

Traveling Proctologist/Mexican Spy

END TRANSMISSION - SNXBLORT

✉

SUBJECT: Re: Own your own shopping mall!
TO: Dixy
FROM: Jonathan Land <jland@incomplete.net>
DATE: 12/11/2002

I just discovered a remarkable new way to make money on the Internet and thought you might want to check this out for yourself. The company is called SmartMall.Biz.

Someone I highly respect and admire sent me a link to their marketing site to take a look, and within a few minutes, I began to realize the enormous poten-tial for making some serious money.

I think you might agree that this is quite extraordinary! SmartMall.Biz is giving away free beautifully designed personalized shopping malls that actu-ally have the look and feel of a real mall. They look absolutely amazing! You have to see it to believe it. If you or anyone you know likes to shop, then you're going to love this program!

SmartMall.Biz just recently launched this program and is about to release a major ad campaign. I highly recommend that you grab a position immediately! It's 100% Free to register, plus, you get a Free Personal Marketing Site to refer others to. You have nothing to lose and everything to gain!

Please check it out for yourself.

By the way, if you ever wanted to get in on something at the top, THIS IS IT!

Dear well-intentioned entrepreneur,

I'm afraid I'll have to pass on your offer. In the creation of your digital "mall," it sounds like you're forgetting the all-important social aspect of a physical mall. For instance, I'll be arsed if any one of your clients has a decent food court, restrooms, a big-name department store like Sears or J.C. Penney, or a multiplex complete with ne'er-do-well teens congregating outside, smoking cigarettes as if they were old enough to buy them, while gossiping about "who likes who" and waiting for a good parking lot fistfight to take place.

What I'm trying to say here is that a day at the mall is an essential American cultural experience that simply can't be replaced by technology, particularly for the children. I live in Kingston, NY, right near the Hudson Valley Mall. It's pretty much the only mall for miles. Kingston's an interesting place. All the residents are either 17 and younger or 40 and older. I'm an aberration in my late 20s. I'm too old to run with the army of teens and too young to be their father. I'd like to think I fulfill a special role here, particularly at the mall, where I've taken on the role of being an unofficial guidance counselor. The kids you have aimlessly wandering around your Web mall on a Saturday night aren't in the environment that will help them become adults, merely consumer shut-ins.

Sure, it's not all positive down at the proper mall. One time I was wearing a checkered button-down shirt and jeans, looking extremely nerdy to the youngsters, when one of them passed me by and said, "Dude, I think you left your pocket protector at home," to which I replied, "Actually, I probably just left it at your mom's house last night." His friends then laughed and enjoyed the quip enough to restrain him from pummeling me. Sometimes the kids merely cough "*freak*" as they walk by me, just before I trip them.

Yet there are experiences in the mall that are amazingly rewarding and essential for these kids' character building. These cannot be taken away from today's teens! Let me tell you a story that started on a Friday night many months ago that proves my point.

I was buying cleaning supplies at Target and checking out. I saw a new register opening up, and I darted to it with my shopping cart at full throttle, causing as few casualties and as little property damage as possible. The cashier's name was Judy (according to her helpful name tag), and she was just finishing up a conversation with her boyfriend.

"So my parents went away for the weekend. Why don't you come over so we can finally . . . you know . . ." proposed the suave lothario.

Judy giggled coyly, "OK, I'll be there after I get off at 10."

Even though it was a sex thing, it was very sweet and innocent. She kept her eyes fixed on the boy as he walked out of the store.

I broached the subject tenderly, "You two are a cute couple."

She let loose a blushy smile, "Thanks."

"So tonight's the big night?"

She turned bright red, "Yeah."

"First time? For both of you?"

"Yeah."

I smiled and tried to be helpful, "Well, have fun. I don't need to give you a lecture about protection, right?"

She broke into what looked like a sunburn. "No, we're all set. Thanks."

"Okay."

As I was signing my credit card authorization, a serious question was raised in my mind.

"Listen," I said, "I would feel irresponsible not telling you this, but as someone who's slightly older, slightly wiser, and has been around the block enough to pass 'GO' and collect $200 several times -- not literally, of course, no one's ever paid me for sex -- there's something very important you should know about losing your virginity. Something that They don't tell you."

"What?"

"It's really going to suck. Not necessarily in a painful sort of way, although that's not out of the realm of possibility, but because both of you have no idea what you're doing it'll be just awful. Seriously. I guarantee you that the following exchange will occur, initiated by one or the other of you: 'Is it in?' 'I'm not sure.' 'How about now?' There's going to be an absence of the appropriate amount of foreplay, misdirected from the appropriate places to a brief amount of kissing, and gratuitous breast manipulation. Then the ill-prepared thrusting begins. Just take it slowly, and make sure you're both ready."

"Gosh."

"I don't mean to offend you in any way, but such is the way of life, so try not to build this up into some big thing. You won't orgasm, and it'll be a logistical nightmare. Sex truly gets better with experience."

"Thanks, I'll remember that . . . really."

"Good."

Then I decided to do the right thing and help out a teen in need.

"Now, this might sound a little strange, and I'll preface this by saying this: I'm not hitting on you. I'm merely providing a valuable life service for someone in need. So here it goes: Like I said before, I'm older, and wiser, and I know what I'm doing. If you want to have proper sex with someone who can show you more or less what it's all about, I'm up to the task."

All of a sudden there was a violent change in her demeanor: "Get the fuck out of my business you fucking creep!"

"God, I thought you might take that the wrong way. Here, I'll give you my phone number and address just in case. Please think about it. I'm seriously just trying to help. I don't see you as a hot, shapely, naive young girl, just as a blooming flower who needs a good watering with a powerful hose. Wait, that didn't come out quite right."

"GET OUT OF HERE!!!"

I did. Quite quickly at that. I put my purchases in my car, trying to figure out where I went wrong, to no avail. I then drove around to the movie theater. That side of the mall was hopping.

I was thinking about seeing a comedy, when I noticed a group of four goth kids being refused admittance into the latest horror movie. I stepped in and tried to be more helpful with a more trivial matter, as opposed to taking on the hard and heavy issues of mere minutes before.

"Excuse me." I queried the cashier, "What seems to be the problem here?"

"These kids have no ID. I can't let them into an R-rated movie."

"I see. Well, I'm their legal guardian. I've allowed them to go see the film."

He wasn't buying it. "Do you have any proof of that?"

"I'm not in the habit of carrying around documentation of my children's relationship to me, but I can fill you in on their lives before I adopted them."

I pointed to the one closest to me. "Nancy here is the daughter of two trapeze artists. One time they were performing as part of a circus troupe when a rival group of entertainers wheeled into town. They loosened the safety net before one of Nancy's parents' performances, and then blasted a large noise during it. The usually dexterous acrobats lost their concentration and fell to their deaths. The sinister clown responsible for the whole thing felt the pressure of the large shoe of the law, but wound up getting off scot-free.

"Mark's mom was a trucker. She was doing a run up to Albany, with her husband along for the ride, when all of a sudden about 15 deer made a run for it across the thruway. She managed to squash all but one of them like bugs on the grill of her 18-wheeler, but the last one was in midair and was hit in such a way as to send the creature crashing through the windshield, with one branch of antlers decapitating each parent. Poor Mark had to ID the only head they could find.

"It took me a little while to discover William's origins. After starting a fight in school, I spanked him. He was crying, but frankly I wasn't even putting all my weight into it or following through. I found out he killed his single dad with a knife after a spanking. He was a pro tennis legend. The only reason why he didn't kill me is because an open-palmed slap is nothing compared to the mighty power behind a two-handed backstroke, so to speak.

"And last, but not least, is Cindy. Of course, I would much rather have been spanking this former child beauty queen. Her parents were tangled and strangled in their own elaborate Christmas lighting display three years ago. To be honest, the G-rated "The Santa Clause 2" would be much worse for her to see than the goriest slasher flick you could show her.

"Now, I hate like hell for the kids to be forced to hear all of this and relive the pasts they're so bravely attempting to move on from, but it's just to prove the point to you that any fictional trauma is a cakewalk to these kids."

The cashier was moved. "OK, will you fucking stop already? They can go, but you have to go in with them. Holy fucking shit, can you talk!"

"Please, the language . . . not in front of the kids."

We all went in. They were very thankful, and they thought that I was a good guy. I learned their real names, and I also gave them my phone number and address in case they ever needed anything, before I sneaked into another theater where I could actually keep my eyes open and fixed upon the screen without the intimidation of brutal, extensive gore.

Later that night there was a knock on my door. I figured that the girl from Target had thought about what I said and had come over for a somewhat clinical, educational, yet thoroughly enjoyable introduction into the world of sexual experience. I opened my door to find Judy, but apparently she brought her entire high school football team with her. They beat me up pretty severely, drank all my booze, and then beat me up again, just when I was about to figure out how I was going to get to the hospital without the use of my broken hand to either drive there or call an ambulance. I tried to get them to stop, but they wouldn't. Drinking, that is. It was difficult to see, between the blood in my eyes and the wincing from extreme pain, but there didn't appear to be a designated driver in the bunch!

Luckily, the police arrived to detain these hooligans. It would appear that the kids from the movie also came over to hang out, saw what was happening to me, and called the cops. I'm proud to have made up an elaborate lie about how they were my children. After the cops rid my apartment of the Kingston High football team, my Kingston High goth squad carried me like an invertebrate blob downstairs and got me the medical attention I so richly deserved.

When I came to, I was extremely disoriented. "What time is it?" I asked. "It's 9 a.m. . . . on Monday. We hung around all weekend to be here if you needed anything." Rebecca (aka Cindy) said.

"Thank you, that's very sweet. Shouldn't you kids be in school?"

"Yeah, but we didn't want to leave you alone."

"I appreciate that. Well, maybe you should go, and if one of you wouldn't mind taking turns feeding me through a straw and changing my catheter during lunch and after school, I'd pay you for your efforts. You're a good bunch."

"Don't worry, man; it's the least we can do."

After about a month they wheeled me into Target for some shopping. When we checked out, the clerk was, you guessed it, Judy. I apologized about the little misunderstanding when we last met, and she apologized as well. She said she figured out that I wasn't such a bad guy after all if I could take the goth kids and make them happy under my tutelage. She also confirmed my fears for her first sexual encounter, which is when she informed her football player boyfriend about what I had said and my offer, right before he rallied the troops to kick my ass. As a peace offering, she gave me her employee's discount. Unfortunately her boyfriend was visiting her right at that moment.

Later that night, the football team kicked in my door, and beat the living tar out of me again. I attempted to reason with them, but they weren't seeing my point, so they broke my jaw. Still feeling that I could get through to them, I crawled over to a pad and pen to finish my sentence, but then they started working on my arms. In a last-ditch attempt, I was trying to scrawl out an apology in my own blood on the carpet. That's when Judy showed up. However, this time Judy wasn't there as a wicked observer enjoying her besmirched honor being restored through force. She actually figured out what the team was up to and came to my house to stop it after what felt like only 8 or 9 broken bones this time. I was very proud once again.

Judy called up my goth friends and told them what was up with me. She got me to the hospital, and the goths met up with us there.

Sometimes life gets messy, and these kids need to learn that. If it weren't for these occurrences in the mall, kids would never learn about the things that kids need to learn about. Sure, I could have done without the emotional and physical wear and tear, but the net result made me happy enough to endure the pain of smiling, even if it meant popping the pins out of my jaw.

Judy learned about sex, trust, and the ills of violence. The goth kids learned ... well, I'm not sure what they learned, but they definitely seem more upbeat and positive than they were when I met them. Steve (aka William) now even wears a BEIGE trenchcoat! The entire football team missed its games for the following week because they were all in jail. I hope they've learned their lesson as well, along with one or two unintentional ones, such as how essential lubricant is to anal sex, particularly with large felons.

So there you have it. I mean no ill will, but I hope your business fails miserably, because if you succeed, it is our children who will fail.

Jonathan Land

Unofficial Guidance Counselor

Hudson Valley Mall

SUBJECT: Re: Your Child Can Read with Ease!
TO: Dinophonics <Barry@emsemail1.com>
FROM: Jonathan Land <jland@incomplete.net>
DATE: 04/19/2004

Hello Fellow Educator,

I have the most difficult job in the world. You're probably thinking: "Who the hell are you, the President of the United States?" Close. I'm his Speech Therapist and Tutor.

I desperately require your service because I think it's my last shot at success. I've tried everything from standard coaching, and then taking regressive steps towards high school textbooks, grade school textbooks, and finally Little Golden Books and the "Read With Dick and Jane" series. Dinophonics . . . you're next! Now, I'm not saying that the President is completely illiterate or unable to think on his feet. The unfortunate fact is that his brain doesn't process external or internal information in a reasonable, logical way. Whether it's his days of coke and booze, the undiagnosed Adult Attention Deficit Disorder, or his penchant for huffing rubber cement, I don't know, but whatever cognitive thought processes the man has are defeated by an inordinate number of misfirings between the neurons in his brain. While I truly believe that this massive and constant source of randomly-fired energy could power a small city (I've seen him turn a light bulb on in his mouth like Uncle Fester from "The Addams Family"), it makes both expressing himself and understanding his own thoughts an uphill battle to say the least. That's why they called me in . . . "the expert."

Obviously, you've seen my work, and most people would say it's unimpressive. Believe me, I'm as disappointed as the rest of the world, but in my defense, I have my hands full. I have worked with the mentally and physically disabled for nearly 30 years. You'd think that dealing with a man-child of marginal intellectual faculties due to undetermined brain damage would be a cakewalk for me! Hell, I've taught brain-dead kids in iron lungs how to play the harmonica! Actually, all you need to do is stick a harmonica in their mouth, but it's still a crowd-pleaser.

Alas, I have discovered that you can lead a jackass to the waters of literature, but you can't make him sip from the cup of knowledge, even when offering a beer chaser. I'm almost glad, in a way. If Bush were to sip from a cup of knowledge, his backwash would taint the rest of us with infectious stupidity.

I've brought Mr. Bush to the Library of Congress on many occasions, and all he's interested in is feeling the texture of old leather-bound tomes . . . with his tongue. He calls it "getting learned by osmosis." While I'm proud that he knows the word "osmosis," I am ashamed of his particular lack of understanding of the concept. If only saliva was smarts. . . .

My work with George W. Bush makes Anne Sullivan's education of Helen Keller look like a college refresher course, and not the "miracle work" it's touted as.

This horrible and embarrassing failure will look awful on my resume. I would have quit years ago, but I thought: "This will be my greatest triumph ever! I can't pass up an opportunity like this. I will become the toast of educational circles around the world, and I'll make millions off of my future tell-all book: 'From Duh to Dominance of the English Language,' and its follow-up 'Intelligence for Dummies.'" Nowadays I think: "Jane Goodall will be able to get one of her subjects to give a coherent speech before I can!"

Just to give you an example of what I'm dealing with, here are some excerpts of transcribed recordings I've made of the President. As part of my work with him, I've planted a tape recorder on Mr. Bush, with his permission, so I can go over things with him such as presentation, diction, composure, and the literal definitions of words. I've had 3 transcribers suffocate to death, choking on their own laughter after reading this material.

Excerpt 1: 9/10/01 — Private discussion with Condoleezza Rice and Donald Rumsfeld

Donald Rumsfeld: . . . So like I was saying before you took your "Little Georgie" break. We have the "terrorists" fly the planes into the Twin Towers. We also have two more planes target the nearly empty wing of the Pentagon and crash another in a field somewhere as a distraction. We'll claim that one's headed for D.C. too. Operation Al Queda is a win-win situation. You will get to claim the greatest victory over the greatest adversity America has ever faced, and you off some money-grubbing Jews in the process. Re-election is guaranteed, and once we strong-arm the bill killing term limits through, you will be President until you kick the bucket.

President Bush: Can I fly one of the Twin Tower planes? I'll glide that sucker smack-dab in the middle of the building, then ride off into the sunset on my trusty horse!

Condoleezza Rice: I don't think you'd want to do that, Mr. President.

President Bush: Why not?

Condoleezza Rice: Because you'll die, sir.

President Bush: I thought that becoming President granted me Special Powers!

Condoleezza Rice: Not those kind of powers, sir. Have you been reading comic books again, sir?

President Bush: God damn it! I need some coke!

Donald Rumsfeld: We're really getting off track here.

President Bush: I really can't fly a plane into the Twin Towers? Not just one of them?

Donald Rumsfeld: Listen, Mr. President. If you're good, when we start the war you can put on the fighter pilot costume you love so much, and land a plane . . . that's land . . . not crash . . . on an aircraft carrier.

President Bush: I made a number two in that uniform last night. It smells poopy.

Excerpt 2: 9/11/01 — Whispered discussion with Secret Service Agent

Secret Service Agent: Sir, an airplane just collided with one of the World Trade Center buildings.

President Bush: Was it a paper airplane? How far did it go? Mine never go far.

Secret Service Agent: No, sir. It was a commercial airliner.

President Bush: I don't care what people say. I love commercials.

Secret Service Agent: Focus, sir.

President Bush: Ah yes. I see. OK, which world's Trade Center was hit?

Secret Service Agent: Uh . . . the one in New York City, sir.

President Bush: Isn't New York on Earth? I might not be the brightest brick in the belfry, but even I know New York isn't a planet. You should really read your horoscope more often to learn about the country's galaxy. You might get learned a thing or two.

Secret Service Agent: What?

President Bush: I'm going to wait for you to get your story straight and if something happens here on Earth, in the American part, I'll pounce into action like a wildcat with its tail caught in my bum.

Secret Service Agent: I give up. [mutters] Assclown.

President Bush: I love clowns!

[. . . later . . .]

Secret Service Agent: Sir, the second of the Twin Towers has been hit.

President Bush: Why would someone punch a building? Did the guy get hurt? Was it a Federal building? Can we be sued? Wait. Didn't I OK that?

Secret Service Agent: Huh? No, sir. The second of the two Twin Towers of the World Trade Center was hit by another commercial airliner. Definitely a metal plane. I can't imagine you authorized this unless you're the personification of pure evil.

President Bush: Nah, I talked to God this morning, and he thinks I'm cool. Hmm . . . World Trade Center you say?

Secret Service Agent: Yes, sir.

President Bush: Which world?

Secret Service Agent: Actually it's just a name, sir. It's in New York City . . . which is in New York State . . . which is one of the United States . . . of which you are the President.

President Bush: I forget . . . which states in America are united?

Secret Service Agent: All of them, sir.

President Bush: Even Hawaii? They seem a bit standoffish.

Secret Service Agent: Yes sir, even Hawaii.

President Bush: Well, it looks to me like they're trying to secede. Location, location, location. We need to bring this situation under control. Has anyone thought of bombing them?

Secret Service Agent: It's already happened, sir.

President Bush: Did we do it?

Secret Service Agent: No, the Japanese did.

President Bush: Really? Should we thank them or bomb them back?

Secret Service Agent: We already bombed the Japanese, sir, with two nuclear bombs.

President Bush: That'll show 'em. How come I wasn't briefed on this?

Secret Service Agent: It happened over 60 years ago.

President Bush: Still, shouldn't I have approved it?

Secret Service Agent: You weren't born yet, sir.

President Bush: Ahhh . . . I can take a hint. You're right. It's best that I don't know about the covert, secret stuff.

Secret Service Agent: We should get back to the task at hand, sir. You know, the terrorist attack on the United States?

President Bush: Ah, yes. I forget . . . which states in America are united?

Excerpt 3: Date unknown — Phone call with Osama bin Laden

Osama bin Laden: So, now do you see the folly of your ways, infidel?

President Bush: You bastard, I've been faithful to my wife! You're thinking of my predecessor.

Osama bin Laden: I don't understand.

President Bush: Understand this, Assclown, I'm going to take you downtown! I'm going to float like a butterfly, sting like a bee, and I'm the chocolate that's going to melt in your mouth and not in your hands, bitch.

Osama bin Laden: Such noble diplomacy! Why don't you come over here and say that?

President Bush: I got my diplomacy from Yale. It's hanging on my office wall! You name the time and place, and I'll be there, stretch. No, wait. I'm in control here. I'll name the time and place!

[silence]

Osama bin Laden: You still there?

President Bush: Wha . . . what was I saying?

Osama bin Laden: You wanted to fight me.

President Bush: Yeah, I'll come over to Iraq and fight you mano-a-mano.

Osama bin Laden: Iraq? If you say so.

President Bush: I'll meet you in the schoolyard at 3, bitch.

Osama bin Laden: I'll be wearing a red turban.

President Bush: Good! It'll match the bloody pulp I beat you into, Hussein.

Osama bin Laden: Umm, I'm not . . . you've got to be kidding me.

So there you have it.

Like I said before . . . I really think Dinophonics is my last shot at developing the President's mind to a functional, quasi-adult level. Given what I've described . . . can you give me an assessment of whether or not your program will be able to help in this situation?

Jonathan Land (but I like to go by "Alan Smithee")

The President's Speech Therapist and Educational Tutor

The White House

Warning/Disclaimer: Do Not Try This at Home (Or Anywhere Else You Have an Internet Connection)

Unless you're planning on writing a book like this one, the last thing you ever want to do is reply to spam. You don't even want to click on a link asking if you want to unsubscribe, because the probability of that actually happening is slim to none.

When you reply to a piece of junk e-mail from a disreputable source in any form, your action simply acknowledges that you have a live e-mail address. The spammer will take this information and use it to sell your e-mail address to many more spammers. And then you'll get more spam.

Just to give you an example: When I first started replying to spam, I got about 5–10 pieces of it in my in-box a day. I now get 400–450 pieces of spam a day. On the one hand, I appreciate all of the source material. On the other . . . I'll never get to use over 99 percent of it.

Don't let this happen to you.

Here are some excellent resources containing information about how to deal with spam. May they serve you well:

The Spam Primer:

http://www.spamprimer.com/

GetNetWise:

http://spam.getnetwise.org/

How to complain to a spammer's Internet Service Provider:

http://spam.abuse.net/userhelp/howtocomplain.shtml

JunkBusters:

http://www.junkbusters.com/ht/en/junkemail.html

Urban Legends Reference Pages: Inboxer Rebellion:

http://www.snopes.com/inboxer/inboxer.htm

STEAL THIS COMPUTER BOOK 3
What They Won't Tell You About the Internet

by WALLACE WANG

2003, 384 PP.
$24.95, $37.95 CAN
ISBN 1-59327-000-3

This offbeat, non-technical book looks at what hackers do, how they do it, and how you can protect yourself. The third edition of this bestseller (over 150,000 copies sold) is updated to cover rootkits, spyware, web bugs, identity theft, hacktivism, wireless hacking (wardriving), biometrics, and firewalls.

STEAL THIS FILE SHARING BOOK
What They Won't Tell You About File Sharing

by WALLACE WANG & JERRY BULLFROG

SEPTEMBER 2004, 392 PP.
$19.95, $27.95 CAN
ISBN 1-59327-050-X

Steal This File Sharing Book peels back the mystery surrounding file-sharing networks such as Kazaa, Morpheus, and Usenet, showing you how they work and how to use them wisely. It reveals the dangers of using file-sharing networks — including viruses, spyware, and lawsuits — and tells you how to avoid them. Includes coverage of the ongoing battle between the software, video, and music pirates and the industries that are trying to stop them.

THE BOOK OF NERO 6 ULTRA EDITION
CD and DVD Burning Made Easy

by WALLACE WANG

JULY 2004, 264 PP.

$19.95, $27.95 CAN

ISBN 1-59327-043-7

Ahead Software's Nero 6 Ultra Edition is probably the most popular CD and DVD burning software in the world. While it seems like it should be easy to burn CDs and DVDs, burning a CD can be much more complicated than copying a floppy, and many users reach high frustration levels after burning coaster after coaster. *The Book of Nero 6 Ultra Edition* takes you step-by-step through using Nero for various tasks, without the jargon that can make this stuff so difficult. This book adopts a friendly tone and pares things down to what's important, so you won't have to spend your time reading and reading.

THE CULT OF MAC

by LEANDER KAHNEY

SEPTEMBER 2004, 376 PP., HARDCOVER, 4-COLOR

$39.95, $55.95 CAN

ISBN 1-886411-83-2

There is no product on the planet that enjoys the devotion of a Macintosh computer. Apple's machines have legions of loyal, sometimes demented fans. *The Cult of Mac* surveys the devoted following that has grown up around Macintosh computers. From people who get Mac tattoos and haircuts to those who furnish their apartments out of Macintosh computer boxes, this full-color coffee table book details Mac fanaticism in all of its forms.

"If you want to understand what we did, why we did it, and how it worked (or didn't), this is the book to read. It's required reading for anyone who loves his or her Macintosh." — Guy Kawasaki, Mac Evangelist and author of *The Art of the Start*

APPLE CONFIDENTIAL 2.0
The Definitive History of the World's Most Colorful Company

by OWEN W. LINZMAYER

JANUARY 2004, 344 PP.

$19.95, $29.95 CAN

ISBN 1-59327-010-0

Apple Confidential examines the tumultuous history of America's best-known Silicon Valley start-up from its legendary founding almost 30 years ago, through a series of disastrous executive decisions, to its return to profitability, and including Apple's recent move into the music business. This updated and expanded edition includes tons of new photos, timelines, and charts, as well as coverage of new lawsuit battles, updates on former Apple executives, and new chapters on Steve Wozniak and Pixar.

"If you're a member of the Mac faithful or just moderately interested in the company, you simply must buy this book." — MACDEVCENTER.COM

PHONE:

1 (800) 420-7240

OR (415) 863-9900

MONDAY THROUGH FRIDAY,

9 A.M. TO 5 P.M. (PST)

FAX:

(415) 863-9950

24 HOURS A DAY,

7 DAYS A WEEK

EMAIL:

SALES@NOSTARCH.COM

WEB:

HTTP://WWW.NOSTARCH.COM

MAIL:

NO STARCH PRESS

555 DE HARO ST, SUITE 250

SAN FRANCISCO, CA 94107 USA

About the Author

Jonathan Land is an accomplished stick figure artist and a participant in the experimental musical group Negativland. He lives in New York, where he receives about 400 pieces of spam a day.

Updates

Visit http://www.nostarch.com/spamletters.htm for
updates, errata, and other information.